D1084823

A Cajun Girl's Sharecropping Years

A Cajun Girl's Sharecropping Years

VIOLA FONTENOT

Foreword by Cheré Dastugue Coen

University Press of Mississippi / Jackson

www.upress.state.ms.us

The University Press of Mississippi is a member of
the Association of American University Presses.

First printing 2018
∞

Excerpts of earlier versions of this work appeared in *Growing Up in
South Louisiana*, edited by Trent Angers (Acadian House Publishing, 2016).

All photographs are courtesy of Viola Fontenot unless otherwise noted.

Library of Congress Cataloging-in-Publication Data

Names: Fontenot, Viola, 1937– author. | Coen, Cheré Dastugue, writer of foreword.
Title: A Cajun girl's sharecropping years / Viola Fontenot, foreword by
Cheré Dastugue Coen.
Description: Jackson : University Press of Mississippi, [2018] |
Identifiers: LCCN 2017053372 (print) | LCCN 2018000734 (ebook) | ISBN
9781496817082 (epub single) | ISBN 9781496817099 (epub institutional) |
ISBN 9781496817105 (pdf single) | ISBN 9781496817112 (pdf institutional)
| ISBN 9781496817075 (hardcover : alk. paper)
Subjects: LCSH: Fontenot, Viola, 1937-—Anecdotes. | Church Point
(La.)—Social life and customs—Anecdotes. | Cajuns—Social life and
customs—Anecdotes. | Sharecropping—Anecdotes. | LCGFT: Autobiographies.
Classification: LCC HD1478.U6 (ebook) | LCC HD1478.U6 F66 2018 (print) | DDC
976.3/56063092 [B] —dc23
LC record available at https://lccn.loc.gov/2017053372

British Library Cataloging-in-Publication Data available

To my four children who grace my life,
to my four adult grandchildren who enrich my life,
and to my three French-bilingual grandchildren who bring me joy
as they fluently read, write, and speak my beloved French language.

Contents

Contents

Foreword

A hunger in middle school for great reading was sated when I discovered The Little House on the Prairie books by Laura Ingalls Wilder. I ran with Laura through the nineteenth-century prairie hills, skipped over creeks and streams where she and her sister Mary played, and suffered through those frigid North Dakota winters when Laura worked as a young school teacher and her fiancé Almanzo retrieved her on weekends in courtship. I later found American history to be a second love to my career as a writer, but those memoirs of Wilder resonated with my younger self because of its unique feminine voice.

Young girls' lives remain vitally important to documenting the American story but are many times woefully absent from historical accounts. We learn about male heroes and the stories of those who shape and lead our country, but, unfortunately, the protagonists of those stories are mostly male figures. What's also missing are the small, delicate details that define a life: the baking of cakes

on Christmas Eve, dreaming of a cute pair of sandals from a catalog when money is gone, or "pocking" eggs at Easter. Viola Fontenot
not only captures a young girl's history sharecropping on the Cajun
prairie of southwest Louisiana in this charming book, but she gently
takes our hands and leads us into her world, where poverty and joie
de vivre sometimes existed side by side.

I had the pleasure of hearing Viola's stories as the teacher of her
life writing class, where I was engrossed in her early childhood
tales of rural healthcare, the lack of modern conveniences such as
indoor plumbing, and the realities of hard work; I will never look at
a sweet potato the same way again after learning how they are harvested by hand. And even though one feels the intense desire Viola
has of rising above this impoverished state, there's a celebration of
food, music, and dance that resonates through her life and continues
to do so today. Attend any concert by Steve Riley and the Mamou
Playboys, her favorite Cajun band, and you'll find Vi dancing away.

Laura Ingalls Wilder told her childhood and young adult stories
when she needed money during the Great Depression. The books
proved immensely popular, showing readers how life was for pio-
neers on the Western frontier. By the time the books were published,
the Native Americans of the prairies had been removed, land grants
were a thing of the past, and Western cities had been settled and
modernized. How quickly things had changed since her childhood.

Spanning from 1937 to 1955, *A Cajun Girl's Sharecropping Years*
reflects these changes as well, and we peer through the childhood
windows of Viola's simple sharecropping cabin and a set of circum-
stances so different from our own. Today, the cast iron potbelly stove
fueled by wood is no longer used, nor do we have to worry about
carefully adjusting the temperature when cooking. We only turn
a knob. To wash clothes, we must only throw them in a machine.
Illumination magically happens when we flip a switch, unlike Viola's
youth when kerosene lamps were the only source of light. The pleasure of a full bath in a number-three size washtub occurred once
a week, on Saturdays, while hair was washed separately using rain
water captured in wooden barrels.

As she matures, we watch Viola and her family create mattresses from Spanish moss. A community comes together for a *boucherie*, killing and roasting a pig, then spends the day making sausage and other fine foods—with music and dancing, of course. And in Viola's teenage years, when she yearns for the finer things in life a sharecropping income won't afford, she begins a courtship in the Cajun style to a man who will eventually become her husband.

What also makes Viola's stories unique is their location. She and her family grew up speaking Cajun French, a language struggling to survive in today's south Louisiana landscape. Her stories are sprinkled with the lyrical expressions, captured with heartfelt memories so they will last through eternity. If you've ever wondered where those funny expressions come from in Louisiana, here's your chance to find out.

Beneath the charm of westward expansion, there is a thread of pain running through Laura Ingalls Wilder's remembrances. Her father's wanderlust kept the family on the move, and the stress of financial insecurity as well as the constant relocations must have taken its toll on the Wilder family. We feel Viola's pain as well, when those adored sandals—among so many other things—can't be purchased because her father has gambled the money away yet again.

Bravo to Viola Fontenot for allowing us a peek into her childhood, a rare glimpse into the tough sharecropping world of a Cajun family. Like Wilder's books, *A Cajun Girl's Sharecropping Years* should easily become a beloved book for those looking for a unique feminine voice and subject matter.

Cheré Dastugue Coen

Acknowledgments

I am grateful to the University of Louisiana at Lafayette (ULL) for offering and promoting its life writing class for seniors. The classes provided structure to my retirement and opened doors to meet new people. Throughout my life I wrote in journals, finding that the process enabled me to bring clarity and meaning in my life. Writing classes were an easy transition from journaling. That's where I got the inspiration for my sharecropping stories. Beginning with the January semester of 2009, writing continues to be an ongoing part of my life.

Thank you, Mrs. Nancy Colby, my first instructor and facilitator, for your encouragement and interest in my stories. You kept me on the right track. Thanks also to my writing classmates, who were intrigued with sharecropping. They asked provoking questions and encouraged me to dig deeper. I appreciate Linda Domingue and Jane

Gaiennie of my Wednesday French Table, who read my narratives with invaluable critique, editing assistance, and encouragement.

Occasionally I wrote other essays on Cajun culture and a few poems. But the history of my humble beginnings kept tugging me back. I kept writing until I had completed the tale of my first eighteen years in *A Cajun Girl's Sharecropping Years.*

Special thanks to granddaughter Brenna Michael, who first read and commented on my narratives. She provided me with good editing tips, such as using the highlight tool.

I gratefully acknowledge Ernest Stephen Bernard, Ph.D., who critiqued the first two chapters of *A Cajun Girl's Sharecropping Years* in 2011. He provided me with valuable suggestions to improve the manuscript, but I felt overwhelmed and lacked the confidence to do the work, so I tabled the project.

Still, the narratives kept nagging at me, a history lost and gone forever unless I preserved them. During my 2015 semesters of life writing, I embarked on revising the manuscript with attention to detail, structure, and transitions.

Special thanks to Cheré Dastugue Coen for her assistance and encouragement in this arduous task. She believed I could do it.

I am indebted to fellow writer and consultant John Francois for his thoughtful insights on how to make this manuscript better.

Finally, I am grateful to my daughters, who throughout the years put up with my endless references to this undertaking.

A Cajun Girl's
Sharecropping Years

Introduction

Remember "the good old days"?

Most of us have heard that phrase at one time or another. However, my memories of "the good old days" from 1937 to 1955 do not feel so good to me. Sharecropping was still widespread in Louisiana's southern parishes of Acadia, Saint Landry, and Evangeline during the Great Depression and World War II under presidents Franklin D. Roosevelt and Harry S. Truman.

Sharecropping described a poor farmer like my daddy who rented plots of farmland that included a house. The farmer struck a verbal agreement, a *barguine* (bargain), with the landlord. The farmer agreed to pay his landlord a two-thirds share of all the cash proceeds from the sale of cotton and sweet potatoes (the cash crops), and the sharecropper himself got one-third.

Today, sharecropping is mostly history—a bygone era. History is part of who we are, and it plays an important role on where we are going. As part of Louisiana's rich natural cultural heritage, it is vital that sharecropping be documented and preserved.

There are some published sharecropping books; however, they carry a masculine voice and viewpoint, including some stories from African American men. But history should also include the feminine voice, the feminine perspective. Without this aspect, sharecropping history is incomplete.

A Cajun Girl's Sharecropping Years covers that missing link. All in one narrative, it portrays not only the field work, but also the kitchen and domestic arts, as well as Cajun courtship culture and marriage. It is the story of a youthful Cajun girl (*la jeune fille*) who writes, whose voice needs to be heard and find its rightful place in history. It is my personal story of eighteen sharecropping years that revisits my good old days from 1937 to 1955.

My mother, Alice Hébert Doucet (1918–2003), was a descendant from the Acadians of Nova Scotia, Canada, and my father, Lee Joseph Fontenot (1912–1966) was a descendant from French immigrants. Speaking only French (today called Cajun French), they married in October of 1935. Daddy, a bayou man with barely a second-grade education, took up sharecropping near the wooded areas, bayous, and prairies of Richard–Church Point's French-speaking communities in south Louisiana.

I was born on January 7, 1937; my sister Jeanette was born on February 9, 1938; then Betty, March 1939; Lester, April 1942; and Myrtis, November 1946.

A Cajun Girl's Sharecropping Years begins with preschool and the way we lived; then it moves into the first-grade classroom where speaking the only language I knew, my beloved French, was strictly forbidden. My family moved often, and the stories tell how hard and disruptive changing schools was for me. They refer frequently to the mysterious wild woods that captured my imagination. They then chronicle my teenage high school years, the Cajun courtship traditions, my graduation, and my subsequent marriage.

The narratives revisit the domestic life of *boucheries*; days of canning blackberries, figs, pumpkins; laundry; ironing; and making moss mattresses. The narrative brings you to the cotton-picking and sweet potato fields. It ventures into children's French games. Drop in on the joie de vivre of the Cajun holiday traditions of Easter and Christmas. Meander with me through the seasons and cycles of sharecropping via the eyes and life of a young Cajun girl who yearned for better things. And re-examine the myth of the "good old days."

CHAPTER 1

The Preschool Years

We spoke only French, the language of our ancestors, and lived a simple sharecropping life. Our three-room rustic house, without electricity, running water, or a bathroom, was located in the prairies of Acadia Parish near Church Point, stood near a bayou at the end of a rutted farm lane, and was isolated by tall thick woods. I was the eldest of five, the first of three children that were each born thirteen months apart.

A young child rarely remembers a great deal of her early years of life unless a happening was stressful or affected her in some other significant way. The following incidents stand out and remain imbedded in my memory.

Cajun cabin, circa 1840 at LARC Acadian Village.

There were a few times that Mama and Daddy left us alone to play inside the house while they picked cotton in the fields. As the eldest, I watched over my younger sisters.

One particular morning, I noticed that things had gotten very quiet in the cabin. I started looking around for my little sister, Jeanette. I found her a few feet away, slumped on the floor and throwing up. Knowing something was very wrong, I covered her with an old tattered blanket and ran to the fields, yelling for help.

"Daddy, Mama!" I sobbed, out of breath. "Jeanette is very sick." Immediately dropping his cotton sack down in the row, Daddy rushed toward the house with Mama close behind.

Bending over Jeanette, they saw a half-empty kerosene jar near her. The jar was usually stored on top of Mama's kitchen shelf. Shaken and worried, Daddy hastily gathered little Jeanette in his arms and took off running across the field and down the road to get help. He took Jeanette either to a doctor or a *traiteur* (healer), and she remained sick for many days. I recall overhearing Mama and Daddy whispering in low voices that my sister had nearly died. Somehow, I knew I helped save her life.

Following Jeanette's kerosene episode, Mama and Daddy began taking us with them in the fields. Mama made a pad with an old quilt, laid it down in the shade of the wagon for us to play on, and kept watch over us while they worked—hoeing, picking cotton, or digging potatoes.

✤

Daddy—tall, heavy set, and clearly in charge—was a sharp contrast to Mama's short, slightly plump frame and timid demeanor. When he was home, we felt safe and secure. However, he was often away fishing, hunting, and doing sharecropping work.

Alone with her small children, Mama was quick to take notice of any dark clouds gathering across the sky, or lightning flashes here and there, or the rumblings of thunder. Nervous, Mama would dash from window to door, then back to the window again, constantly monitoring the menacing sky. Most times, she suddenly picked up Betty and grabbed Jeanette and me by the hand, and we'd take off running through the fields for protection at a distant neighbor's house. Other times, when Daddy failed to come home at night, Mama became so frightened of the dark shadows that she went to bed and didn't get up until morning. On several occasions, she woke me up to get her a glass of water from the kitchen water bucket. Even though I, too, was afraid of the dark, I did as I was told.

✤

Children who lived on a farm like I did learned early in life that experiencing the loss of an animal or a pet was a common thing, and I was no exception. During my preschool time, I had two pets, a small dog and a baby raccoon. But I learned to let both go.

My little dog was a cute, loveable black and white terrier with a playful disposition. One day when I was about five years old, my sisters and I were playing with him on the porch when he began to act very strange. All at once he jumped to the ground and began running around and around our cabin. Quickly, Mama got us inside the house and locked the doors. As I watched my pet's weird behavior from the window, I saw foam dripping from his mouth. Sometime later he stopped running and was normal again. Mama said my dog probably had rabies, the "mad dog disease." However, feeling the danger was over, she sent us back to play outside.

Mama waited for Daddy to come home from the field. She nervously described my dog's erratic behavior to him. Concerned, he said he had heard widespread stories that the mad dog disease was going around. He told us, "Farm animals, even some creatures of the wild woods, such as squirrels, rabbits, and raccoons, have been seen roaming around with it."

"We'll wait until tomorrow," he said, "and watch the dog to see if he gets another fit."

The next day, Daddy went back to his farm work. About mid-morning, the strange behavior happened again! My dog suddenly went into another running fit. With glazed eyes and foam at the mouth, he ran around and around the house. Once more Mama rushed us safely inside. However, soon it was time for Mama to start cooking dinner, our noon meal, and she needed a bucket of potatoes from the shed. While my rabies-mad dog kept circling the house, she coached me to go get the potatoes.

"I know that you can run out the backdoor to the shed and back inside the house again before the dog returns," Mama said. Although fearful of being attacked, I did as I was told.

Watching the dog run past us, Mama and I stood together in the frame of the backdoor facing the potato shed. Then, urgently, she pressed her hand to my back and yelled, "Run! Run fast to the shed!" I rushed out to the shed, filled my bucket with potatoes, waited, and at her signal dashed back to safety just as the dog once more ran past the door. Shaking and trembling, I handed her the potatoes and fell to the floor.

After the fourth day of fits, my little dog went into seizures and convulsions. I loved my pet, but it was scary to see him acting so bizarre.

"Come here," Daddy called me.

"It's time to do something about your dog. There are no treatments to make him well," he explained in his authoritative, matter-of-fact voice. "He will only get worse. It is best to put him down." Upset and fearful, I watched as Daddy took his shotgun to the open window and shot my tormented pet. Although this seemed a harsh treatment, a poor tenant farmer such as Daddy had no means to pay a veterinarian to put the dog to sleep. A shotgun shell was cheaper.

Repeated nightmares of wild dogs attacking me haunted my sleep for years. And I've often wondered why Mama put me at such risk. In retrospect, I believe that she was simply too young and naive to fully comprehend the danger.

✤

Later, I got another pet. My furry little raccoon provided me with some fond memories. Alone and forlorn, he had wandered into our yard from the thick undergrowth of the nearby wild woods. One day as I sat on the doorsteps of our cabin, he cautiously crept up to me and nuzzled against my legs. With black patches around his eyes and white fur around his nose, he was so cute and cuddly that I quickly became attached to him. After much begging and pleading, Daddy finally allowed me to keep him in the house as a pet.

Returning home one night from our *veillée* (a night visit) to one household down the bayou, we walked into a huge mess! In his playfulness, my pet raccoon had pried open every can of coffee, cornmeal, and flour from Mama's kitchen shelf and spilled the contents all over the stove, table, chairs, and the floors. Baby Coon even managed to rip open the lids from the jars of sugar and lard, which leaked onto the floor, making a sticky paste. I stood near the door with wide eyes, my hand across my open mouth, squirming and cowering away from the chaos.

In a loud, exasperated voice, Daddy said, "You can't keep him anymore. You just can't!" He was upset not only with the scattered jumble but with the lost kitchen staples. "Back into the woods he must go to be with his own kind!" Daddy boomed.

In my heart I knew it was true, but my eyes were sad that night as I watched Daddy carry Baby Coon deep into the dark, mysterious woods. I would miss him, of course, but my heart felt sure he would meet new furry friends and make a new life for himself.

✤

The joyful memories of the Cajun *fais do-do* dances (pronounced "fay-doe-doe") also made a lasting impression on me. Because we had no access to other forms of entertainment, the Saturday night house dances were a regular part of family life and included the whole family and their surrounding neighbors. *Fais do-do* is French for "go to sleep" and refers to the children who accompanied their parents. The mamas put the little ones in beds and on floor pallets made of old quilts in the back bedrooms. Soon after the dance started, the Cajun music lulled the babies and small children to sleep, and the mothers returned to the dancing.

The women danced with each other or with older children if they did not have a partner. I vividly recall one evening Mama danced with Aunt Minnie. My sister Jeanette cried and cried, pulling Mama's skirt, and pleaded for her to stop dancing. I watched as Mama gracefully leaned down with one hand, smoothly lifted Jeanette onto her hip, and without missing a beat, continued to dance.

Daddy customarily played his accordion at these dances. Since my mother's name was Alice, he always played the waltz "Chère Alice" for her. Daddy's own rendition of "Home, Sweet Home, There's No Place Like Home" signaled the end of the dance, and everyone hitched up their ride—wagon, buggy, or horse—and returned home.

Lee Fontenot, playing his accordion, and Chère Alice, circa 1947.

A fais do-do was not only an occasion for fun and social gathering, but also a release from the sharecropper's daily routine of drudgery and hard work.

CHAPTER 2

The Way We Lived: The Way It Was

WOOD STOVE—STAYING WARM—
FAMILY WASH—KEEPING CLEAN

*E*ach day began with Mama cooking on a four-plaque cast iron potbelly wood-burning stove. With a splash of kerosene and the strike of a match, she got the fire started. Wood was also essential for keeping a kettle of water hot to make coffee.

Without a thermostat, the heat on a wood-burning stove was controlled manually. To start a fire, you used the knob on the stove's front door to adjust the air flow into the stove. To regulate the heat and control the smoking, you adjusted the damper (a small oval-shaped metal handle on the stovepipe), which was located at the rear of the stove

Wood-burning stove no. 1. LARC Acadian Village (La Maison Thibodeaux), circa 1820.

and vented through the roof. You turned the handle on the damper back and forth to move a metal plate inside the pipe. When the plate was aligned parallel with the pipe, the plate was at full draw of air flow. When the plate was perpendicular to the pipe, it restricted the air draw.

After Mama started the fire, it didn't take her long to get the heat adjusted. She simply turned the damper handle on the stove pipe a quarter-turn at a time until she had the heat and smoking controlled. She prepared every meal from scratch using her assortment of black iron pots and skillets. She usually made cornbread for breakfast, but sometimes it was *couche couche* (fried cornmeal like finely crumbled cornbread), or biscuits. These were ordinarily served with fresh milk straight from our cow. Other times we put cane syrup over them.

During the warmer months, after breakfast, Mama prepared a fresh batch of bread using a blob of bread dough starter from the previous day. She would knead and mold the dough until it was

Wood-burning stove no. 2. Vermilionville Living History,
Museum and Folklife Park.

thick and smooth, put it in a large bowl, then cover it with a damp
towel. She set the bowl aside on the table for the dough to rise so
it would be ready for cooking with the noon meal. It was too cold
in Mama's kitchen during winter mornings to make bread, as the
dough couldn't rise enough to bake while she made dinner.

Daddy milked the cow every morning for our breakfast and again
every evening for our supper. Our daily fresh whole milk, though
not pasteurized or refrigerated, was quite tasty. I particularly liked

it served warm straight from the milk bucket. And Mama was quite capable of stepping up to do the milking whenever Daddy was not home. At an early age, out to the pasture I went at sundown to round up our milk cow, Jersey. After the milking and feeding she was kept in the barn overnight for the morning milking, then returned to the pasture.

In the spring, our milk did not always taste good. "Woo, ugh!" we sputtered out the awful bitter milk. This happened whenever Jersey got into the bitter weeds, the tall green plants with bright yellow flowers that were so prevalent in the pastures during springtime. None of us could drink that milk! Now what?

Caramel water and PET milk came to the rescue! Mama caramelized one cup of white sugar in her black iron skillet, then added about a quart of water to make a substitute drink until Daddy could get to the store for cans of PET milk. These were "fill ins" for the bitter milk, or whenever we couldn't milk Jersey while she was carrying a calf. Boy, I sure loved that PET milk. One time I sneaked into the supply of canned milk. I hid in a corner, punched holes in the can with a knife, and drank three cans of undiluted PET milk! It was too rich; I got sick with a stomachache and diarrhea and had to confess my misdeed. Mama and Daddy fussed at me, but I felt too bad to care. My sisters Jeanette and Betty always teased me about that humiliating experience.

❖

Dinner was the noon meal. This larger meal was needed to sustain the long hours of outdoor physical work from daylight to sundown. Our everyday dinner staples were meat and potatoes, rice and gravy, and a variety of beans cooked from dry stock. Fresh vegetables came from our farm garden. The meat was often a yard chicken, or maybe meat from a *boucherie*. During hunting season, it could be a rabbit, squirrel, or sometimes a wood duck.

Judging the time by the sun, Mama started cooking dinner about midmorning. With the wood kindling in place, she started the stove fire. Except in winter, the kitchen was always hot, but with the added heat from the stove, it was downright oppressive!

After she lit the stove, she pumped water into the kettle and placed it on the stove to boil. While waiting, she went to the chicken yard, cornered, caught, and killed a chicken by wringing its neck. Working swiftly, she scalded the chicken and plucked the feathers. After cutting up the meat into serving pieces, she washed and seasoned it liberally with salt and cayenne pepper and made smothered chicken. In a deep black pot, she browned the meat in hot lard, then added about one-half cup of water. She cooked, alternately browning and simmering, and added additional water until the meat was almost cooked. Then she added a sliced onion, browned it, and turned over the mixture several times. She continued cooking until the tender spicy chicken with rich brown gravy was done.

Supper, our light evening meal, was usually cornbread and milk, sometimes with a bit of leftovers from dinner. During summertime, Mama often cooked the cornbread stove-top in her iron skillet. She covered it loosely with a lid, and from time to time, carefully flipped the cornbread over to insure both sides were cooked. However, in winter she cooked it in the oven. I liked hot cornbread and fresh milk; both were tasty and nutritious, summer and winter.

❧

The winter cold always got to me. I am full of memories of the misery and discomfort of those days. With little daylight left after school, the rule at home was early to bed and early to rise. When I was about ten years old and after the birth of Mama's fourth child, it became my task to start up the stove fire on school days. Wrapped in a blanket over my night clothes, I shivered as I scuffled my way to the black stove, our only source of heat.

It was tricky to start a stove fire even with good dry wood and a dash of kerosene, but it was a big mess if the wood had the misfortune of being damp. The fire sputtered sparks and smoked with a pungent turpentine-like smell that stung and burned my eyes. The fire stayed sluggish and didn't supply sufficient heat to produce timely hot water in the kettle for coffee or to wash up.

Even with a good fire going, the small black stove could not give off enough heat to warm the room. Our wood-framed houses did not have inside walls such as paneling or sheetrock. In addition, the house was elevated eighteen to twenty-four inches above the ground on wood or bricks pillars. The icy wind whistled through the gaps of the house boards, and more frigid air seeped in between the cracks of the wood floors.

A few times we got lucky, and our sharecropper house had a fireplace for additional heat. However, on school mornings there was no time to start a chimney fire. Besides, no matter how much wood was added, the fireplace, like the stove, only provided heat that reached my face and the front of my body while my backside stayed chilly. I never got used to being cold. But that's the way we lived; that's the way it was.

Our supply of wood came from the endless acres of woods with their assortment of big, tall trees, all within walking distance of our house. It was not unusual for me to catch a glimpse of the backbreaking, monumental work as Daddy's large strong arms swung his heavy ax and methodically chopped a notch around a tree, hour after hour, until it fell. Occasionally, he received a *coup de main*, a helping hand from a neighbor, in using a long cross-saw to cut down a very large tree, but this was rare, as Daddy prided himself on being self-sufficient. Once the tree was down, he sawed it into manageable logs, then loaded these onto the *traineau* (wooden sled), which was hitched up to our mule. Daddy drove the sled back home, then unloaded and stockpiled the logs about four feet high against the side of our house or against the fence. The supply lasted several months.

As needed, Daddy sized the logs to fit the stove. *Chop, thud, chop, thud!* went his ax. Whether it was a sweltering hot day or a cold bleak one, he swung that ax again and again, high above his head, to split the logs and make kindling. Sometimes I watched from my perch on the porch steps. There seemed to be an art in the strength and power of his arms, a rhythm and momentum to it all, as he chopped, carted, and put the wood inside the kitchen door to keep it dry. Since our sharecropping place rarely had a woodshed, I did my share of carrying wood into the kitchen.

Other basics for the way it was: Kerosene lamps and family wash days to keep ourselves clean. The ever-present wagon also played a vital role as it served many needs and was our means of transportation.

Kerosene lamps were our only source of light at night and on dark gloomy days. The lamps were fueled by the same kerosene used to start the stove fire. We usually had three lamps, one for each room in the house. These were refilled every day, the smoky globes were washed weekly, and the wicks were trimmed often. Too long a wick and more soot accumulated on the globes; too short a wick and the flame constantly went out. I was not allowed to help with the lamps as the globes were fragile, easily broken, and needed to be spotless for the best possible light. I well remember spending much time under the dim light of a kerosene lamp, my eyes straining at the books as I read and did my homework.

Saturday was family wash day. Following an early breakfast, the washing took place outdoors. By the time I was nine or ten years old, I was doing this tough and tiring job. For washing and rinsing, two large galvanized number-three size washtubs were used. I

Two kerosene lamps, circa 1820. LARC Acadian Village (La Maison Castile).

placed these side by side on a sturdy work bench in the shade of the house or on the porch.

I hand-pumped water from the well into a *baille-a-pied* (foot-pail) and dumped it into the tubs until they were three-fourths full. The clothes, already sorted by Mama into white and colored batches, were in a pile near the tub. First, I put the white clothes in the water and let them soak thoroughly before I put in the washboard. I rubbed a bar of homemade lye soap or the orange Octagon soap on each piece. I scrubbed them up and down on the old washboard, wrung them out by hand, and transferred them into the rinse tub. My hands and wrists were too small and weak to wring out Daddy's large overalls by myself, so Jeanette helped by grabbing one end while I twisted the other end until most of the water was squeezed out. But instead of staying around to help me hang the clothes, she paired off with Betty and disappeared someplace to play.

Starching our school and dress clothes was part of the laundry process, and these were set aside after the wash. Mama prepared the hot starch by slowly stirring a diluted base of Faultless starch into a pot of boiling water, stirring constantly to prevent it from lumping. She cooked it a few minutes until it thickened like a watery pudding, then removed it from the stove to cool. Mama dipped one wet article of clothing at a time into the starch; as she wrung it out, the wet clothes thinned the starch. She hung these outside with the rest of the wash to dry in fresh air and sunshine.

There was an art to hanging clothes. I picked up a piece of laundry between my forefinger and thumb of both hands, snapped it open to shake out the wrinkles, and laid it over the clothesline. I clipped it in place with clothespins from the small 10- by 12-inch sack that hung around my neck and shoulders. I started with the white pieces, short ones first, then next by size, followed by the colored clothes in the same order. I grouped together items such as washcloths, towels, shirts, blouses, and undies. Sheets and pillowcases took up another clothes line. Last were the pants and overalls.

At about 3:00 P.M., the dry, fresh-smelling clothes were picked off the clothesline, folded as we went, and layered neatly in a clothes basket to be put away—our everyday clothes were not ironed. The starched stiff clothes went into the ironing basket.

Ironing, a tiresome, backbreaking weekly chore, was Mama's job. After I became a teenager, I took over the ironing process with some help from Jeanette. First, I sprinkled water onto each piece of stiff clothing using an old bottle with a cap that had been punctured with nails. Then I rolled each piece and wrapped it inside a towel or a pillow case. The bundles were set aside almost forty-five minutes to allow the clothes to become evenly damp. In the meantime, I put a pair of black irons on top of the hot stove. While waiting for the irons to heat up, I set up our homemade wood ironing board, which was padded with old pieces of blankets or sheets, across the backs of two wooden chairs. From our yard, I cut several twigs from the evergreen cedar tree, placed these at the head of the board, and covered them with a piece of old sheet. I tested the hot irons by sprinkling a few drops of water on them; when the water

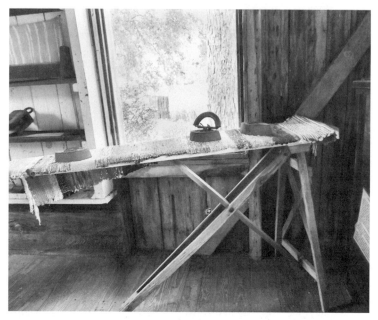

Homemade ironing board, circa 1820. LARC Acadian Village (La Maison Castile).

sizzled, the irons were ready to use. I pressed the iron back and forth over the cedar twigs to clean the black smudges picked up from the stove. This also made the iron glide easily across the damp clothes and adjusted the heat. While I worked, the second iron was left on the stove to make sure it stayed hot.

Ironing, like hanging clothes, had a technique of its own. Pressing down hard on the shirt or blouse, I ironed the collar first, then the sleeves, then the back and front of the body. For a skirt, I began with the length, width and hem, and then ironed the waistband. For pants, I ironed the legs first, then the rest. It was exhausting work that took several hours. The stove, hot irons, and steam from the damp clothes all drained the energy out of me. What a relief it was when we finally got a kerosene clothes iron years later.

❖

Old black wood stove irons, circa 1820. LARC Acadian Village (La Maison Castile).

Keeping clean personally and individually had its routine. Before entering the house, we rinsed our dusty or muddy feet in the foot-pail we kept filled with water near the steps. On weeknights we cleaned up outdoors with a sponge bath using a large dishpan full of water placed on a bench. In winter the sponge baths took place inside the kitchen.

Saturday nights called for a full bath in the number-three size washtub in the kitchen using water heated in a dish pan on the stove. When we were little, the girls were bathed together. But when we were older, each one of us took turns bathing in the same wash water. Hair washing was done separately with rain water captured in wooden barrels or metal drums. I liked washing my hair with lye soap in the rain water; it left my dark hair feeling silky-soft with a glossy shine. Old hand-me-down dresses served as our nightgowns.

⚜

Two other fundamentals of the way it was in sharecropping were the outhouse (outdoor toilet) and the *pot de chambre* (chamber pot). We had two chamber pots, kept under the bed, one in Mama's bedroom and one in ours. When I was nearly eight years old, it was my distasteful morning job to take them outdoors to be emptied and washed, then return them to their places.

It seemed that the outhouse, with its Sears catalog pages as the toilet paper of the day, was also a refuge for my sisters to avoid playing with me.

"Jenny, Betty," I called. "Where are you?"

No answer.

Much louder and pleading, I'd call again, "Jenny, Betty, where are you?"

Still no one answered me! So I went looking for them. Sooner or later I found them hiding in the stuffy, stinky outhouse, whispering, giggling, and conspiring to stay away from me. This left me feeling lonely and rejected. Even back then, it seemed two was company and three was a crowd.

Me and my sisters did evening chores such as gathering eggs from the hen house, which at times housed ducks, geese, and turkeys. We shucked and shelled corn, usually one bucketful, to feed the chickens and added a handful of corn to the hogs' food scraps. Shelling the hard, dry, jagged, and dusty corn kernels was a sure recipe for red fingers and blisters on my tender hands. Daddy took care of feeding the larger animals: the horses, the cow, the calf, and the hogs. There were times when he bought feed in bulk from the country feed store, and it was so much easier to measure out a bucket of feed than shelling dry corn.

Feed, flour, and sugar were bought in bulk in ten-, twenty-, or fifty-pound cotton sacks that came in different colors and prints, which were suitable to make dresses. The trick was to buy two or three sacks with the same pattern to have enough material for one outfit. Mostly, Daddy wasn't able to get matching sacks, but a few times I got lucky. On those occasions, I was overjoyed with the idea of getting a new dress!

Although Mama didn't sew, Aunt Lena did. She was my dad's sister and my *marraine* (godmother), and a good seamstress. She and her family lived near us for a year or two. I have kind memories of the two or three pretty feed-sack dresses she made for me. Once,

Inside of outhouse, circa 1820. LARC Acadian Village (La Maison Thibodeaux).

for my birthday, she even made me a new dress from store-bought material of light green with a small flowery print. The dress was so pretty, with a one-and-one-half-inch ruffle sewed across the bodice and on the sleeves. Other than that, my dresses were mostly hand-me-downs that rarely fit this skinny little girl.

Although the way we lived was hard, that's the way it was. In my heart, I hoped that my young life would get better once I started school.

CHAPTER 3

First Grade—Moving— Moss Mattress

"I will not speak French on the school ground anymore."
A permanently lodged first grade memory.

When I was six years old, it was with some anticipation that I entered first grade in September of 1943 at Richard Elementary. The small rural school was located on Highway 370, about fifteen miles west of Church Point in Acadia Parish.

On the first school day, Daddy walked me down the bumpy dusty road (*p'tit chemin*) to the bus stop. That day he also made arrangements with a neighbor who lived near the bus stop for me to wait in their home on cold or rainy days. Other than that, I was on my own.

I was anxious about walking by myself to the bus stop. The road rambled about a mile around rows of depleted cotton and sweet potato crops, which were now used as pastures for the farm animals. Shrouded in early morning fog, the towering horses and big cows looked so menacing, and I was plagued with fears that one of them, or maybe a stray dog, might have rabies and start chasing me. During the afternoon's return walk, I felt that there were tall dark shadows peering at me from the underbrush of the large trees.

I went to school barefoot and wore clothes passed on to me by my aunts and cousins. For winter, Daddy bought me a pair of boy's ugly brown high-top work shoes. I felt so ashamed wearing those shoes. The dreadful things had big thick soles with leather shoe strings that laced through eyelets up the foot then fastened around metal hooks at mid-calf.

Wearing used dresses and going barefoot or wearing my ugly high-top shoes contributed to my feelings of isolation and intimidation at school. I was shy and spoke only French. But speaking French on the school grounds was strictly forbidden. Trying to make myself understood was embarrassing. I felt belittled by the teacher's disapproving frowns, stern looks, and squinting eyes. Her superior attitude undermined my self-esteem. In general, the school teachers' attitude toward Cajun culture made me feel ashamed and second-rate, as if speaking French was a bad thing or a stigma. Although I wasn't the only one who spoke French, each time I was caught speaking it, my teacher instructed me to stand in front of the whole class while she whacked my hands with a ruler or ordered me to write one hundred lines of "I will not speak French on the school grounds anymore." Sometimes she assigned both punishments. It was meant to disgrace me! In spite of all my teachers' efforts to exterminate my French language and my heritage, I soon figured out it was in my best interest to keep both French and English, one for school and one for home and family.

The naturally proud, stubborn, and clannish French-speaking Acadians resisted any attempts to become "Americanized" by the English-speaking community. "Les américains," Daddy said, "want

us to give up our language, our music, and our way of life." He didn't
like *les américains*. And he wanted to be left alone to live his simple, uncomplicated life in harmony with the land, the endless wild
woods, and the bayous.

I don't recall having any special friends during first grade. But, oh,
I had the magic of books: readers, spelling books, arithmetic books,
and storybooks of fairy tales and nursery rhymes! All these became
my good friends; they opened up a whole new world to me—one
that I had no idea existed. After first grade ended, I felt my days were
meaningless.

But September soon returned, and I eagerly awaited second
grade. I expected Jeanette, now six, to accompany me to the bus stop,
and begin first grade.

But that was not to be!

"Mama, I do not want to go to school without Betty," my sister
wailed, morning after morning. Mama quickly gave up the hassle of
Jeanette's crying fits. It was easier to keep her home as a companion
to Betty and to keep watch over our brother, Lester. In any case, my
parents did not consider getting an education a priority. Although
disappointed, I now had a small measure of confidence as I walked
to the bus stop.

Alone, I started second grade.

Even knowing that speaking my beloved French would not be
allowed, I looked forward to learning more about reading, writing,
and doing numbers.

Secretly, my heart yearned for a pair of girls' shoes. Soon after I
started second grade, I worked up the nerve to ask Daddy for them.
Timidly, I approached him.

"Please, Daddy," I said, "this year, would you buy me a pair of girls'
shoes and not those brown high-top boys' shoes?"

He listened but didn't say much. Then, a few weeks later and quite
unexpectedly, Daddy came home and handed me a box. Surprised,
I opened it and found a pretty pair of shiny, low-cut black patent
leather shoes with a narrow strap fitting across the foot to buckle

on the side. Oh, what a delight to have my first pair of Mary Jane shoes! I ignored Daddy's reminder, "Now, don't wear the new shoes on rainy days. Use the brown high tops on the muddy road." I was deaf to his every word and promptly put on my new shoes. Beaming with pride, I went skipping up and down the room. I couldn't wait to wear them to school!

The next day when I wore my new shoes, I could feel the admiration of my classmates. School was the place to be, that's for sure, and being a good student helped me fit in better. That year I even made a few friends.

Gradually, I became aware that my younger sisters were almost inseparable. They were thirteen months apart, both had blond hair, and they looked alike. Some people even thought they were twins. I was different, the dark haired girl, and the one who had been separated from them during first grade. I was also the one who kept her nose in a book whenever possible.

⚜

We spent early summer and most weekends visiting our grandparents. Besides going to school, that was one constant enjoyable part of my life.

Rarely did we visit Pop-Pop Fontenot since he lived alone following Mémère (grandma) Fontenot's death. She had died when I was six months old, so I never knew her. Pop-Pop Fontenot's homestead, located a few miles north of Church Point on Highway 1108, was close enough for us to walk for an occasional brief outing. A few times we took a wagon trip to go see one or two of Daddy's brothers and sisters, who owned their own farm nearby.

It was Mama's family, the Doucets, that we frequently went to see. Although we didn't attend church, most Sunday mornings Daddy hitched the mules to the wagon, and off we'd go, the mules trotting down the dusty gravel road to Mom-Mom and Pop-Pop Doucet's farm in the Branch community of Acadia Parish. They had a large family of thirteen children. During my school years, eight were married with children of their own, and four lived at home, farming with Pop-Pop Doucet. Our many aunts, uncles, and cousins regularly joined us there for a noontime Cajun dinner at Mom-Mom's and we visited all day, speaking in our customary Cajun French. Occasionally these get-togethers turned into an afternoon of back-porch Cajun music.

After breezing through second grade, I eagerly anticipated third. However, come September, Daddy and Mama were in the middle of cotton-picking time and needed extra hands. Harvesting the crops came first. Since I was eight years old, Jeanette seven, and Betty six, we were deemed old enough to become part of the labor force—the much-needed additional pairs of hands. My sisters and I did not start school just yet. Instead, the three of us worked with Mama and Daddy from sunup to sundown in the cotton rows. It was an accepted practice that farm children were kept out of school until most of the crops were harvested. At last, almost four weeks into the new school year, Jeanette and Betty entered first grade, and I started third. I was happy to finally have my sisters' company to the bus stop.

We moved almost every year. I was dismayed and frustrated at the same lookalike three-room house, always located at the end of a bumpy lane, near a wooded area and a murky bayou. Even though our new place was still in Acadia Parish, my school records indicate that I switched elementary schools three times, from Richard, to Branch, then onto Church Point.

❧

Our sharecropper houses each had two bedrooms; Mama sparsely furnished both of them with a brown chest of drawers and a double-sized bed with an iron-spindled headboard. The beds were fitted with wire-coil bedsprings and topped with homemade moss mattresses.

My sisters and I slept three, and later four, on the double-size mattress with its squeaky bedspring. As long as we were young and little, or it was winter, it was alright, but as we got older and bigger, we had to sleep sideways. In summer it was downright crowded. Without fans or air conditioning, it was hot and aggravating! Our discomfort and jarring elbows and knees usually prompted a round of giggles and arguments between us.

"Arrête ce train—stop that noise," hollered my mother from her bedroom. We quieted down a bit but soon started up again.

"Arrête ce train asteur! Stop the noise now!"

Most times, no amount of scolding would shut us up. Suddenly, Mama would be in our room; she had had enough. *Slap! Slap!* went the fly swatter as she spanked our legs. Sure enough, the spanking ended the arguments and, crying, finally we fell asleep.

The moss mattresses required yearly cleanings. Come May or June, early in the morning under a clear blue sky, Mama, my two sisters, and I hauled the two mattresses outdoors into the shade of a large tree. Using sharp scissors, we ripped open the seams of the ticking, the dust flying all over us as we grabbed and pulled out the squashed, lumpy moss and piled it on the ground. We washed the ticking in a galvanized washtub and hung it out to dry.

Next, my sisters and I cleaned the moss. We sat cross-legged on the ground in a semicircle around the piles. For several hours, we grabbed bundles of moss between our hands, pulled and pried them apart, shook out the dust, and fluffed them, then set them aside in the sunny, breezy air to be rejuvenated. It was a gritty, dusty job. Strands of moss got all over our hair and clothes. Black moss powder covered our faces, arms, and legs, and we sniffled and sneezed from breathing in all that stuff! Our backs and arms ached from pulling and sifting.

Finally, we took the dried ticking of both mattresses and hand-stitched three sides closed. We divided the restored moss in half and by handfuls stuffed it back inside the ticking, spreading it evenly, then stitched the fourth side. The two mattresses were so heavy and bulky that it required four of us to lug one mattress at a time back onto the bedsprings.

At last, weary and filthy, we headed for an outdoor washtub bath behind a corner of the house. Not one, not two, but three tubs of bath water were used to wash off all the dirt and grime.

Old wagon, circa 1820–90. LARC Acadian Village, Lafayette.

One year, we needed to make a new moss mattress. So Daddy hitched our mules, Carroll and Jerry, to our wagon. Jeanette and I sat in the bottom of it as he drove it deep into the thick woods to find a wild oak or hickory tree with Spanish moss (green moss). With his pitchfork, Daddy pulled the green moss down from the branches and loaded it in the wagon while Jeanette and I spread it with our rake until the moss was layered about sixteen inches thick.

Back home, Daddy unloaded the Spanish moss into a pit and wetted it down to begin the curing (decay) process. Once a week or so, he turned it over with his pitchfork until the moss turned black. For our limited need of only one mattress, the curing process took about four months. Larger, deeper pits of green moss could take up to six or eight months to cure.

Cleaning the new cured moss took long hours of intensive work. It was a backbreaking, dirty process. One by one we plucked out all the rooted bugs, insects, sticks, twigs, dried bark, leaves, and any weak broken fibers. We pried and shook out the dust and fluffed it up and spread it in fresh air with sunshine for several hours before we made the new mattress.

Corn shucks were occasionally used as mattress fillers. For a short time, I had a corn shuck mattress. It was noisy, lumpy, and prickly. Each time I moved, the mattress dipped and made crunchy sounds. I was relieved when it was replaced with a moss mattress.

✝

Between school, the cotton rows, and moss mattresses, we did enjoy some moments of reprieve with the "Watkins Man."

Daddy was the one who went to the store for supplies, so my sisters and I never got to visit a store. We were always delighted when Mama said, "Here comes the Watkins Man." (The Watkins Company was founded in 1868 by J. R. Watkins of Plainview, Minnesota. The company is still going strong today, and you can find some Watkins products at Wal-Mart and Target.)

The Watkins traveling salesman was a colorful character of farm life. We cheerfully awaited his store-on-wheels, "the hack," as we called his truck. He came about one a month and seemed to know everyone, sharing news of neighbors and other tidbits.

He sold all kinds of merchandise and Watkins products, the usual cans of baking powder, baking soda, salt and pepper, and assorted fine extracts of vanilla, banana, and root beer, along with bottled spices such as cinnamon, nutmeg, cloves, and more.

The Watkins Man, also the local medicine man, stocked many remedial items. There were salves of all kinds. Some were used to heal cuts and draw out splinters, others relieved the dry, cracked udder of a milk cow. There were home remedies such as liniments, rubbing alcohol, and astringents used to treat burns, rashes, sunburns, and other skin ailments. Some of these products were used on both people and animals. He carried face lotion and bleaching creams, guaranteed to remove brown spots from the face and hands. During that era, a clear white skin was a source of pride. In fact, girls and women alike wore a *garde-soleil* (Cajun sun bonnet) and home-made hand mittens with open fingertips to pick cotton, or anytime they were outside in the sun, to prevent tanned skin, freckles, and brown spots.

I particularly recall the rosebud salve that Mama bought for our cracked lips and dry hands. The soft, pink salve smelled and tasted like fresh roses. The small round tin can, about the size of a fifty-cent coin, had a wreath of roses with an "R" in the center; the salve is still available today in specialty gift stores. Once, Mama bought a tin of rosebud salve just for me. I felt special because this time, I *did not* have to share.

Best of all were the many varieties of sweet goodies. The ones I remember best are the peppermint sticks and the rainbow coconut candy bars, now found in the candy section of many stores. But the short-lived visit of the Watkins Man did not long distract me from the isolation of my sisters' tight bond or our yearly move.

Sharecropping and making moss mattresses weren't the only labors that me and my sisters provided. We also helped gather and prepare a variety of foods for the table.

CHAPTER 4

Food Affairs

BOUCHERIES—CANNING

As sharecroppers, my sisters and I lent our extra hands to prepare and keep food on the table.

Boucheries, canning, and preserving foods were common undertakings during the late forties until the mid-fifties, when we didn't yet have access to electricity. Similar to a co-op, a boucherie was a gathering of farmers, neighbors, and family who came together to butcher hogs, or maybe a calf. The boucherie provided the group with fresh meat for two or three days and rotated from one household to the next on a weekly, bimonthly, or monthly basis, depending upon the agreement.

Daddy and Mama were part of a boucherie and participated in the strenuous adult work. My role as a young girl was limited. However, I listened and observed the boucherie activities and helped whenever I was needed.

Sometimes a man did not have a pig to butcher but worked as an extra hand in exchange for a share of meat for his family. A lot of precision teamwork went into a boucherie. The fast-paced hard work took place on a cold winter day, which prevented the raw meat from spoiling. The brisk cold air was an energy boost to the working party. Boucheries also served as a social affair, where friends and neighbors visited and exchanged news as they butchered, prepared, and preserved the meat. The practice continued even after electricity was brought to the farms of Acadia Parish.

The day before the event, each man prepared the tools of the trade, which included sharpening all varieties and sizes of knives. For identification, a family often dabbed paint on their tools. A couple of men placed several large, black cast iron pots at the butchering site. Nearby, piles of wood were gathered, cut, and stacked high so the fires could be kept going all day.

The boucherie members gathered outdoors at daybreak and drank many pots of strong black coffee throughout the day. They filled the black pots with water and built huge roaring fires under them and brought the water to a rolling boil. The hogs were slaughtered and scalded in the hot water, and the hair was scraped off.

They formed work groups and hustled and bustled in an easygoing but orderly manner. All day long, you could hear the friendly banter between them. Two or three men constantly added logs and wood to the fires. Another unit carved the meat into different cuts: larger ones into pork chops, ribs, or roasts, and small boneless pieces for the meatgrinder. These were all set aside to be divided between the families.

One unit made *grattons*, or cracklings, a delicious snack, hot or cold. With long sharp knives they cut strips of pork skin and a band of meat, usually from the belly, into cubes. The Cajun cooks filled a black pot about one-quarter full with water placed over a sizable fire and brought the water to a boil. They dropped a few gratton cubes into the water, which melted the fat as the water evaporated to fry. More cubes were dropped into the pot as they continued. The grattons were deep-fried to the right stage, then scooped out of the hot oil with an oversized, long, slotted ladle and dumped into large galvanized dish pans. While still hot, the grattons were sprinkled generously with salt and cayenne pepper. Frying grattons went on for hours.

After the grattons were done, the hot oil rendered from the meat cubes was allowed to cool until it was safe to handle. Using a metal dipper, the oil, now soft lard, was poured into gallon jars, capped tightly, and partitioned among the members. Lard was the basis of most Cajun cooking, including making roux, browning meat, frying, and making cornbread and biscuits, a big part of everyday meals.

I tagged along as Mama joined a group of women, watched as they worked, laughed, and joked, and kept fresh coffee on the stove. The young children stayed near their mamas or slept on the floor upon quilts, while the older ones were shooed outdoors to play.

I helped pump water into pails and carried these to Mama's group as they cleaned the pigs' intestines to be used as casings for the *boudin* and sausage. The women poured copious amounts of water into the intestines, then emptied them; they washed the casings this way four or five times. Vinegar, used as a disinfectant, was added to the final rinse. The cleaning continued until every part of the hog, which included the head, ears, and the feet, was done.

I looked on as Mama's unit began the boudin preparations. I helped a pair of women wash and chop onions, parsley, and garlic by the bucket. Some was used to cook dinner, and lots of it was used to make boudin, hog head cheese, and sausage. Bony cuts of meat and the head were cooked in seasoned boiling water, deboned, and minced for making boudin. One lady ground small chunks of boneless meat to make the stuffing for sausages and the *panse* (the cleaned, stuffed, and later smoked stomach). Meat grinders had special tubing attachments that enabled a person to fill the casings with boudin or sausage mix.

A team of women prepared the noon meal. Sometimes the cooks made a *bouillie* (a heavily seasoned clear soup) with the liver, heart, kidney, spleen, and other bits of meat tossed together with plenty of onions. Sometimes they made a *fricassée de reintier* (backbone stew), or other times they made a *roti de reintier* (oven rib roast). Dinner was served on a rotating schedule without interrupting the work.

Certain cuts of meat were preserved with a heavy coat of rock salt and allowed to cure in large crock jars as salt pork and slab bacon. Other meats, like *tasso* (strips of meat roughly three inches wide and eight inches long) were sprinkled with plenty of salt and cayenne pepper and smoked alongside the sausages and the *panse*. Tasso was used to season beans, stews, gravies, and gumbos.

Most farmers had their own smokehouses—outdoor sheds about the size of an outhouse with metal pole racks running from one wall to the other to hang the meat. If not, you could team up with a family who had one. In addition to smoking the appetizing meats from the boucherie, during the hunting season, the smokehouses were used to smoke wild game such as rabbits and ducks.

Smoking meats was an acquired art and needed a watchful eye for several days to get it right. Heavier woods like oak and hickory worked best. If the smoke became too hot and smoked the meat too much, it became dry and chewy. On the other hand, if it wasn't smoked enough, the meat quickly spoiled, and all was lost, including the many hours of hard work. Sometimes, smoked sausages were layered in a circle in a crock jar and covered with hot lard to extend preservation.

At dusk, the final cleanups complete, the families loaded their wagons with their belongings and their share of meats and headed home. Although the cold morning activities began in a jovial social mood, everyone returned home somber and exhausted.

⚜

The seasonal canning and preserving of fruits and vegetables was another way of keeping food on the table. Blackberries and figs, delicious fresh or canned, were plentiful and free for the picking and a core staple during winter.

Louisiana has many varieties of figs. I was most familiar with the small and medium purple ones. Our sharecropping houses usually had at least two fig trees, which were often located in the backyard, or near a corner of the house. If there were none, the neighbor down the road had some to share. Fig picking typically began in late June and continued through mid-July.

At sunrise, after our usual breakfast of cornbread and milk, we dressed in raggedy long-sleeve shirts and skirts or hand-me-down pants, and we tied a kerchiefs around our heads and underneath our hair. We slipped on handmade open-fingered mittens, which shielded our hands from the sun and the sticky white gummy sap that oozed from the plucked figs!

We picked the ripened figs every two or three days in the cool morning. Daddy positioned the ladder against the trunk of the fig tree and waited on standby for the filled buckets. One by one, me and my sisters climbed up the ladder and cautiously shinned up the tree. I braced myself between a sturdy fork of branches with large prickly-palm-like leaves. I held the pail in the crook of my left arm as my eyes scanned for clusters of purple sun-ripened figs. I glanced down at Daddy, whose authoritative demeanor strongly conveyed, "Start picking!" Focused on the task, I extended my right hand and began. Picking figs was a dull, sticky, and monotonous job, not given to playfulness. I skipped the bird-pecked and over-ripe fruits and picked until my pail was three-fourths full. I inched down the ladder and handed my cumbersome pail of figs to Daddy, who emptied it into a large washtub, or gumbo pot. In a sort of assembly line, he handed the empty pails back to me and my sisters as we moved from one niche to another and onto the next tree, until the awkward and tedious picking was finished.

Weary and sweating from the late morning sun, I rid myself of my scratchy, itchy clothes, as did my sisters, and we washed up. After a quick change of clothes, we gobbled down a glass of milk and a biscuit topped with figs before we returned outdoors to clean the figs.

Daddy met us near the tubs, which he had carried to the water pump and filled with water.

"Let's get the figs washed," he said. We sat around the tub and worked through two rinses and carefully avoided mashing or bruising the figs. The first rinse was used to float up the leaves and twigs, which were poured out. During the second rinse, we cut off and discarded the stem of each fig before we placed it into the cooking pot.

Mama started the canning process by filling two eight- or ten-quart pots about three-fourths full of figs. She put these pots on the stove, and though Cajun cooks did not measure, added nearly two quarts of sugar per pot and covered the figs with three or so inches of water. She brought that to a boil, and with a watchful eye stirred occasionally to prevent sticking. Mama let the figs simmer until the juice was a thin syrup and ready to be canned.

In the meantime, Jeanette and I washed mason quart jars in hot soapy water, rinsed them shiny clean, and inverted them on a clean towel to dry. About ten minutes before canning, Mama put a new box of lids and rims into a pan of slightly boiling water for sterilization and sealing.

Mama ladled the hot figs into the quarts, covered them with one inch of syrup, and left another inch of air space under the lid. Quickly, she cleaned the mouth of the jar with a warm rag, grabbed her tongs, slapped a hot lid on the jar, and closed it tightly. Jeanette and I took over and wiped down each quart and placed it on the kitchen table to cool. Once the cooling process began, I heard the rhythm of "ting, ting, ting" going off day and night as the lids sealed. I inspected each jar the next ten days for signs of spoiling before they were stored on a shelf away from sunlight.

The first canning yielded about two dozen quarts, followed by smaller batches of one dozen, then tapered off to a few pints. Figs were often doled out with biscuits or with fresh baked bread and a glass of milk, but fig cakes and pies were my preference.

⚜

Barely three weeks separated the fig canning from blackberry picking. I recall picking some in late May from the wild, straggly,

Canned figs, circa 1820. LARC Acadian Village (La Maison Castile).

blackberry bushes scattered along our ditches and fences. We ate some fresh from the pails; the rest Mama made into tasty cobblers or blackberry dumplings. Other times we ate the berries sprinkled with sugar and cream spread over her hot homemade French bread.

Our yearly canning of blackberries came from the acres of nearby dense woods. Daddy selected a picking day in late June or early July, when he knew that almost one-half of the large, juicy berries would be ripe.

After an early breakfast, we clad ourselves in the same manner as we did to pick figs, though we added a straw hat. To ward off redbugs, each of us tied a strip of cloth dipped in stinky, oily kerosene around our ankles. Daddy hitched our mules to the wagon and loaded it with an assortment of buckets, picking pails, large washtubs, and a jug of water. All geared up, we climbed in and set off for our blackberry-picking rendezvous.

From his hunting excursions, Daddy knew that many thick blackberry bushes surrounded the tall pine, hickory, and oaks trees that were hidden deep in the woods. Upon reaching such a spot, Daddy handed us our pails, while he carried the larger buckets. He paired me with Jeanette, his two eldest, and paired younger Betty under his leadership, as his loud voice instructed us, "Allons se dépêcher et finir avec ça! Let's hurry up and finish with this!" Nodding our heads "yes," and mindful of snakes, we treaded cautiously around the bushes and began picking.

My clothes were soon damp from dew and sweat and sticky with berry juice. In spite of long sleeves and mittens, I couldn't avoid the burning scratches of the long, pesky, thorny vines. I was petrified of hornets and the red and yellowjacket wasps! Their nests were hidden deep in the bushes, and I considered myself lucky if I escaped with only one sting.

An hour or so later, Daddy's loud voice interrupted my thoughts. "Dépêche, dépêche, allons finir avec ça avant ça fait trop chaud! Hurry up, hurry up, let's finish before it gets too hot!"

"Ouais," we all responded in one tired voice.

Four pairs of hands worked steadily, and the tubs were usually full by 11:00 A.M. Hot, dirty, and hungry, we scrambled into the wagon and headed back. At home with my little brother, Mama had dinner ready for us. We washed up and changed clothes, then ate.

Following a brief rest, I joined my sisters for the cleaning process. We washed the berries the same way as figs. In the first rinse, the twigs, bugs, and dead leaves floated to the top, and we scooped these up with a strainer, then discarded with the dirty water. During the second rinse, the green, brown, and hard berries were ladled up and thrown away as the water drained. There was a third and final rinse before Mama started canning.

She put several large pots of blackberries on the stove and added the sugar. Mindful that berries released their own juice, she used less water, then simmered them until done. Mama's secret to tasty blackberry dishes was a sweet, strong, berry-tasting juice, not watered-down and weak. The blackberries were canned the same way as figs.

Oh, yes, that night we usually had a worthy treat—delicious blackberry dumplings for supper!

Achingly tired, I washed up and crawled in the bed with my sisters, only to be kept awake with aggravating, burning itches. Somehow, the teeny irritating redbugs had managed to overcome the kerosene rags and lodged themselves around my ankles, behind my knees, and in the groin area. I couldn't stop scratching, and the welts turned red and formed scabs. The misery lasted almost eight days.

Our sharecrop house rarely had a pear tree, but Daddy bought one or two bushels from the fruit stands. The pears were tough to peel and slice, but being larger than figs or berries, the work went faster. We got about a dozen quarts of canned pears each year.

❧

And then there were the okra and the pumpkins.

Daddy grew about ten rows of pumpkins. Preparing pumpkins for canning took hours of wielding a sharp knife. The tough skin was hard to peel, and cutting the firm flesh into cubes caused painful blisters on my hands. Fortunately, the cannings were spaced several days apart.

Pumpkins took longer to cook. Mama simmered the cubes until cooked, but still firm, in a slightly thick syrup base. About thirty minutes before canning, Mama added spices and orange rinds, or a variation of one cup of shredded coconut or crushed pineapple. The quarts of bright orange pumpkin looked and tasted nothing like the mashed bland stuff you find in cans today! Pumpkins added a tangy taste to biscuits and made colorful, delicious pies. Once in a while, Mama made specialty treats of watermelon rind preserves and a cucumber relish called "chow-chow."

❧

We harvested okra every other day to avoid the hard and rubbery stalks larger okra yielded. Daddy and Mama were in the rows of okra plants by 6:30 A.M., where they cut the okra and placed them in a large bucket. Like figs, okra is covered with fuzz that causes acute itching on your hands and between your fingers. Me and Jeanette put on long-sleeve shirts and mittens to wash off the fuzz with a clean, damp cloth. We lined up the okra stalks two at time on a clean flat surface, and using a sharp knife, we cut off the tips, then sliced the okra in quarter-inch pieces and put these into large dishpans.

Mama seasoned the okra with salt and pepper, and she used a large long-handled spoon to transfer the sliced okra into hot cooking oil in her black iron skillet. She made "smothered okra." She turned the okra over and over until it lost its sticky film and cooked it until it turned slightly brown. She folded one-half cup of sliced onions into the okra and turned over the mixture another fifteen minutes. Last, she stirred a freshly diced tomato into the pot and cooked ten more minutes. She added a tablespoon of water as needed to obtain the desired consistency and adjusted the seasoning. The smothered okra was served over hot rice or as a side dish. To make chicken and sausage okra gumbo or dried shrimps and okra gumbo, she simply added a quart or two of warm water to the smothered okra. After electricity reached us in Acadia Parish, Mama cooked batches of smothered okra and laid it flat in quart bags in the freezer, always ready for a quick meal.

⚜

Our large farm garden had an assortment of vegetables. My sisters and I helped gather and harvest vegetables such as tomatoes, sweet peas, green beans, and Irish potatoes, as we called the white potatoes. I snapped and shelled different kinds of black-eyed peas, sweet peas, and purple hull peas. There were rows of watermelon, cantaloupe, and squash to be picked. Included in the garden were the staples of Cajun cooking: green onions, parsley, and a variety of peppers, onions, and garlic.

Working to keep fresh food on the table was a part of sharecropping. Further reflections bring other glimpses into that past.

CHAPTER 5

Glimpses down Memory Lane

THE GRAND OLD HOUSE—SWEET POTATO VINES—
ELECTRICITY AT LAST

Our move into the grand old four-bedroom house was special, even though we only had furniture for three rooms. I was about ten years old and treasured living there for one whole year. Its drab paint-peeled appearance boasted a hint of grander years. The once nice wood floors were faded, scratched, and neglected, and the large elongated kitchen boasted its own fireplace, as did the spacious vacant parlor room to the left of the kitchen. For once, I caught the bus at the house—no more long walks, and this time I did not need to change from the school of my previous year. The grand old house was located on a gravel road off of Highway 95 in the Pitreville (pronounced "Peetville") area, about ten miles north of Church Point, Louisiana.

The barren round room held my imagination with its unusual hexagon-shaped walls and many tall windows, and I felt that some sort of mysterious air floated in the room! I envisioned it with the fine furniture of its time, fitted with lovely drapes. The room became my favorite place to play, and I dreamed that I lived in such a fine mansion with my own private bedroom. I fantasized that I had pretty dresses with shoes to match, didn't go barefoot anymore, and never moved again!

That's the place where I saw snow for the first time. Everything stayed frozen for two or three days. We ran out of indoor wood, and our outdoor stacks were wet and frozen. Daddy was unable to keep a fire going in the fireplace, and our only heat came from the short-lived fire in the cooking stove. The cold immobilized me, and for two days me and my sisters stayed in bed and kept warm under piles of blankets and quilts. I was so glad when the sun came out!

This time we had neighbors that lived close enough that I could see their house. Elkins was their last name, and I became friends with a girl my own age. It was fun to have a girlfriend to visit and play with on Saturday or Sunday afternoons.

❧

In the introduction, I explained that a sharecropper's barguine was a verbal agreement between the sharecropper and his landlord. Daddy's agreement with the landlord stated that the landlord received two-thirds of the cash proceeds from the cotton and sweet potatoes, and Daddy, in compensation for his and his family's farm labor, was allowed one-third of the cash.

In order to help Daddy get started, the landlord set Daddy up with two charge accounts, one at a grocery and a second one at a feed and seed store. It was Daddy's job to make sure that the year's credit charges would be less than his one-third share. He charged the necessary feed, seed, and fertilizer for spring planting, and only essential groceries like flour, cornmeal, coffee, lard, and sugar, and occasionally PET milk. Daddy's barguine further emphasized that both charge accounts had to be paid in full before he got any money. And Daddy gambled that after he paid out both charge accounts, he would have some cash to buy us clothes and shoes.

Mindful of the farming almanac and based on his past experiences, each spring Daddy began the tough work of preparing the land for planting. With only basic farm implements, at sunrise, he hitched his mules, Carroll and Jerry, to a plow and got started. In a few weeks, he had cultivated several acres into field patches with long neat rows. Eight or ten rows were set aside for our vegetable garden, and the others were assigned to sweet potatoes and cotton.

"No seeds will sprout if planted on Good Friday," I heard Daddy mutter with an ominous look. Every spring, I heard that same prediction. It seemed that it was a taboo—no one should disturb the soil on the days Jesus laid buried in the ground. On numerous occasions during a thunderstorm, I overheard his grave pronouncement, "Le Bon Dieu est fâché. The good God is angry."

Was it superstition or reverence?

Mom and Dad were nonpracticing Catholics; still, they had us all baptized within two weeks of our birth. By the time we were age seven, they made sure that someone picked us up, or that we walked, to religion classes. My siblings and I made the sacraments of First Communion by age eight and received Confirmation by age thirteen. Mama taught us the rosary prayers in French, even though praying the rosary was not practiced at home. But at Mom-Mom Doucet's house, it was a family ritual to pray the rosary out loud every night, *en français* and on our knees, whenever my sisters and I slept over.

⚜

Undoubtedly, Daddy often wished his three short girls were tall strong boys. Being a young skinny girl, I lacked the strength and stamina to plow, cultivate, or plant cotton seeds. As I wrote in chapter 3, I was in the third grade when I first worked in the fields side by side with Mom and Dad. By midspring, Daddy had finished planting the cotton seeds. Now it was time to plant the sweet potatoes. First, Daddy planted several "mother rows" of sweet potatoes. In a week or so, the buried potatoes sprouted with vines. Several weeks later, the vines draped profusely about thirty-six inches down the rows. Daddy designated the day after a drenching rain a "planting day." Early in the morning, when the vines and rows were still wet, Daddy used his razor-sharp knife to cut the "mother" vines into strips eight to ten inches long. He layered the vines in the wagon and drove it to the sweet potato field.

Straw hats on our heads and barefoot, dressed in long-sleeved standard field wear, my sisters and I joined Daddy at the wagon of vines. He handed each of us a planting fork he had carved and fashioned from pieces of wood or from forked tree branches. The two-pronged fork resembled a sling-shot. The handle was about six inches long; the prongs were about one inch apart and four inches long. I grabbed a handful of dripping wet vines in my left hand and positioned the fork in my right. Head down, bent at the waist, I placed one vine at a time across the middle of the soggy row and pushed it down four inches deep in the soil, then shoved a blob of mud over the vine to close the hole. Vine by vine, I continued to plant, placing each vine ten to twelve inches from the last.

It was laborious, muddy work. In the morning, my feet sank into the black squishy mud, and it oozed between my toes! By midafternoon the mud had dried stiff and irritated my feet, and I had to wash them in a water hole before I could keep working. By late afternoon, painful blisters had formed in the palm of my planting fork hand. Mama put a rag pad on the blisters, tied it with a strip of cloth, and I stayed on the job. We hurried to do all the planting while the soil was moist. Two days was all the time we could take to get it done.

Once, I ventured enough nerves to ask, "Daddy, would you please buy me some gloves?"

Tipping his head to me, he boomed, "Ils coûtent de trop pour acheter à crédit. They cost too much to buy on credit." I stuffed my feelings inside and kept working. That evening, it took two washtubs of water to get cleaned up. Exhausted, I ate my supper and went straight to bed.

We had two or three weeks' reprieve between planting and hoeing. First, Daddy hoed and thinned out the cotton plants. Two weeks later, Jeanette and I were back in the fields, clutching long hoes with razor-sharp blades. Daddy monitored and cautioned us, "Do not cut or damage the young plants, as you are cutting out real money!" It was precision work, and we had to keep our eyes on the hoe and the plants. "Chop, chop," we shaved the grass and weeds that invaded the young cotton and sweet potato plants. Two weeks later, we did a second hoeing. At last, the spring field work was finished; we were free for part of the summer.

✢

The phrase "Daddy liked to play cards and liked his whiskey" is etched in my memory. Between seasons, and on weekends, Bourré was his game of choice. The card games were held at a neighbor's house or in the back room of a bar or at a nightclub in town. A tall and portly man, he dressed in his denim overalls, a plain long-sleeve shirt and a cap, and off he went. He walked to the neighborhood game. He hitchhiked if the game was in town. Either way, he left us alone some nights and many weekends.

I don't remember him drinking at home, but I remember one incident when he got back home and insisted that I wash his feet in a dishpan of water. I was intimidated and hesitated, but Mama nodded for me to do so, after which he silently went to bed. He wasn't hurtful to us, but I often overheard Mama fussing about the money he lost at bourré. No matter, he never stopped.

✢

It was 1948 or 1949, and the talk was going around! I was about twelve years old and in the sixth or seventh grade, when I heard that electricity was headed for south Louisiana. Towns, cities, and our schools had electricity, but no one wanted the expense of electrifying the rural areas. President Franklin D. Roosevelt created the Rural Electrification Administration (REA) in 1936 to bring electricity to farms and rural prairies by providing interest-free loans to co-ops, and local and state governments. Financed by REA loans, distribution cooperatives were formed to erect poles, string lines, and install transformers throughout those areas.

The South Louisiana Electric Membership Corporation (SLEMCO) was the co-op formed in south Louisiana that finally brought electricity to Acadia Parish. I well remember the event.

"I see them," I hollered to my sisters, who were out of view.

"See what?" they called back.

"The men," I said as I jumped up and down.

"What men?" they asked, looking around as they approached me.

"The ones with the electric poles!"

I waved in the direction of the men who were plodding through the fields and across our pasture toward our house, surveying and marking the spots with little red flags. They unloaded several big trucks of equipment and supplies along the way.

I was transfixed! For more than an hour, time stood still.

Leaning against an old fence post, spellbound, I gazed at the workers as they dug holes, erected poles, attached transformers, and strung heavy coiled wires down the mile or so to our house. At last the work was complete and a string of poles and power lines forever dotted the farms and pastures of Acadia Parish.

Finally, one of the SLEMCO crew wired our house on behalf of the landlord. Eager and excited with anticipation, I barely slept that night.

What an event! The next day, an electric cord about two feet long, with a light bulb at the end, hung down from the ceiling in each room of our house. Although I was accustomed to electricity at school, it was pretty heavy stuff to have it at home. Mama saved the kerosene lamps for an emergency, and with glee, I pulled the chain in our bedroom for a bright light, ready to read and study.

That year, after the harvested crops were sold, Daddy bought three things: a wringer washing machine, a large deep freezer, and unexpectedly, a battery-operated radio. The freezer doubled as a part-time refrigerator for milk and leftover foods as long as these were monitored and removed before they froze. The wringer washing machine was highly prized over the washboard laundry chores. And I, as did my sisters, loved the Saturday night "Grand Ole Opry."

❖

It is unclear to me when I first realized that Mama suffered from painful kidney stones and bladder infections. Back then, parents rarely allowed children around grownup conversations, and we were no exception. Vaguely, I remember that Daddy mentioned a few times that Mama's left kidney "was sick," and some days she didn't work with us.

I was about thirteen years old during the summer months of 1950 or 1951 when Daddy told us that Mama needed an operation and that the doctors had already given her an appointment at the Charity Hospital in New Orleans. My sisters, Jeanette, Betty, and Myrtis, and my brother Lester and I, each with a small packed bag, climbed into the wagon, and Daddy brought the five of us to live at Mom-Mom and Pop-Pop Doucet's farm until Mama was well. He explained that she would stay in the hospital a few weeks, and it might take a long time before she got better.

Daddy didn't have a car, nor did he drive. I learned later that he had made certain arrangements with a truck driver from Shuff's Truck Stop, Savoy Community (located off of Highway 190, east of Eunice).On the arranged date, the truck driver picked up Daddy and Mama at Shuff's and drove them to the Charity Hospital in New Orleans. There, Mama had major surgery, and her doctors removed her stone-damaged left kidney. She remained in the hospital several weeks before she came home.

That event changed many things. Mama recovered slowly, and she tired easily. Fortunately, she never again suffered from kidney stones

Three-burner kerosene stove, circa 1820. LARC
Acadian Village (La Maison Thibodeaux).

or bladder infections. The doctors warned her to avoid any laborious work that placed a burden on her remaining kidney. Field work was considered too strenuous, so Mama didn't work in the fields anymore. She always reminded us that it was crucial for her to drink water throughout the day for her remaining kidney to work properly and stay healthy.

Even though nobody talked about it to us, I picked up pieces of conversation that said Mama's bad kidney had been punctured with so many little stones that it was on the verge of rupturing. What I did notice during the rest of her life were the deep scars and indentations that ran about two or three inches across the top of her left arm. I overheard that the pockmarks were caused by the shots and intravenous medicine injected into her arm during her surgery.

For the next six months, Jeanette and I swept, mopped, and scrubbed the wood floors in addition to doing the laundry and ironing. Shortly after Mama's operation, Daddy bought a three-burner kerosene stove to make things easier for her.

Electricity, a freezer, and a kerosene stove certainly improved our sharecropping life. But some things still evaded us: a car, indoor plumbing, and a phone. And yes, there was more backbreaking work to be done: picking cotton and digging sweet potatoes.

CHAPTER 6

Show Me the Cash

PICKING COTTON—DIGGING SWEET POTATOES

The words "paying cash" were highly praised by the Cajuns. The words "charged on credit" were considered a disgrace.

Cotton was our number one cash crop. The cotton bolls opened and were ready for picking about mid-August, with the season in full swing through September.

At daybreak, the humidity high and muggy, me and my two sisters washed the sleepiness out of our eyes and had a breakfast of cornbread and milk. Dressed for field work in long-sleeved dresses or shirts and pants, we put on our *garde-soleils* and tied the strings under our chins. Barefoot and holding our cotton-picking mittens,

"Going to Gin." Felix Soileau, circa 1950. Courtesy of D. J. Soileau.

we carried a jug of summer-tepid water from the well. Before Mom's surgery, we trailed her and Dad to the cotton fields as the yellow glow and heat of the rising sun greeted us. My young brother Lester, and later my younger sister, Myrtis, were placed on an old quilt to play in the shade of the wagon. Other times they followed behind Mama.

At the cotton rows, we were handed gray striped cotton-picking sacks. These store-bought sacks were made from heavy cotton twill ducking. Mama altered them to fit our height by securely hand-stitching a double fold at the bottom, which allowed the sack to drag about two feet behind us. The doubled bottom provided extra protection from tears made by dragging the heavy cotton-filled sacks over roots, sticks, and stones. I looped the strap around my neck and under my shoulder and adjusted it with a knot, then put on my mittens.

Picking Cotton. Mr. and Mrs. Felix Soileau, circa 1950. Courtesy of D. J. Soileau.

Now it was time to start! My sisters and I were small and short; Daddy paired me and Jeanette (the two eldest, stronger girls) on each side of one cotton row. A strong picker, Daddy paired with Betty, and Mama picked with young Lester in tow. This way, three rows of cotton were picked during one run.

The tall plants, boasting fluffy snow-white cotton resembling golf balls, were also dotted with many hard green bolls (*les grabots*) waiting to open up in next weeks' sunshine. The opened cotton clusters had mean pointed burrs that pricked my hands and fingertips.

The bushy cotton's green hand-shaped leaves, wet with morning dew, quickly dampened my sack and made it heavier. Along the cotton rows, the leaves were covered with speckled crawling caterpillars who were waiting for me. Next came the invasion! Within thirty minutes the fuzzy worms had sneaked onto my sleeves and decorated my shirt. Some resembled miniature black and gold tigers, others were rainbow colors of blue and green, and the rest were a varied assortment of black, gray, and white. Long and short, fat and juicy, the worms crawled up my neck and inside my collar. Queasy and disgusted, I slapped at the creepy things to dislodge them, which only made things worse. The squashed mucus was now smeared on my skin and my clothes.

By 11:00 A.M., the broiling sunrays assailed my back. First it steamed my clothes, then dried them and left them smelly and starch-stiff. The hot, humid stench of the squashed worm mucus insulted my sense of smell. No matter, I wiped my hands on my skirt and kept at it.

Bending low, I used both hands to reach for the white cotton and picked that plant clean, and dragged my sack to the next plant. By the end of the row my sack was full and weighed about twenty-five pounds. I straightened out my aching back, took a deep breath, and wiped the sweat from my face. Between sips of warm water, I emptied my sack in the side-railed wagon and started on the next row. The only interruptions were a thirty-minute rest with noon dinner and brief water breaks. At last I became aware of the slowly receding sun from the bright blue sky. I stood up, removed my *garde-soleil*, and felt the slightly cooler air around me and breathed, "Merci, Bon Dieu—thanks, good God."

Day after dirty, stinky, hot day, me and my sisters worked with Mama and Daddy. My back screamed for its normal upright position. My hands and fingers, jabbed by the burrs, were bleeding and sore. My feet were dry, cracked, and burned from walking on the hot, hard dirt clods between the rows.

Squabbles erupted in the cotton row! Children inevitably find ways and reasons to quarrel. For example, if the stem of a puffed cotton boll was in a neutral position, that is, not facing my side of the row, I stubbornly argued that it was Jeanette's cotton and left it behind. Other times, I sneakily bent stems to Jeanette's side and also skipped those. But Jeanette insisted that these bolls were not hers and didn't pick them. Both actions resulted in a white line of cotton left behind. Sooner or later, Daddy saw the line of puffed cotton, and the 250-pound man got angry!

"Tonnerre m'écrase! Mes petites filles, laissez pas tout le cotton en arrière—do not leave any cotton behind!" he yelled angrily. *Tonnerre m'écrase*, an exclamation of irritation, literally meant "thunder crash." "Si tu fais ça une autre fois, j'vas vous fouetter— if you do that one more time, I will whip you," he continued. Outraged, he went on, "Le coton est notre vie—cotton is our life! Sans ça nous-autres a pas d'argent pour acheter du linge et des souliers—without it, there is no money to buy clothes and shoes!" Hanging my head in shame, I went back and picked every single cotton puff I had left behind. From time to time, we pulled that stunt anyway, but he never did whip us.

By Friday the wagon was piled high with cotton and readied for the gin. Saturday was "gin day." Customarily, it was the man who went to gin. Daddy, being the sole one in our household, got up about 4:00 A.M., hitched the mules to the wagon, and took off. It was imperative to get to the gin early and avoid the long waiting lines. An early start gave him a better chance of getting his cotton ginned before nighttime. During the busiest part of the season, the gin accepted cotton all night. It was vital for us to pick the cotton before a chance rain damaged the fibers.

On Saturdays, while Daddy went to gin, my sisters and I were obliged to keep picking until noon, but often we picked cotton with just one hand while the other was propped on our knee to rest our back. We emptied our cotton into a large burlap gunnysack, but we missed his leadership and fast-picking hands. That afternoon we did the laundry, cleaned up, and waited for Daddy to come home with news of the day. Most times he was back by 8:00 P.M. with big bunches of bananas or bushels of fruit—it was one of the few times that he had cash for treats. On other occasions, he didn't return home until past midnight and didn't have anything.

We were happy when the news was good—our wagon load had yielded an above-average cotton bale and netted a good price. Other times, we were disappointed. The prices had dropped because our cotton had too many seeds and fewer strong cotton-fibers. Often it was due to too much rain; other times it was the poor soil that produced a low-fiber cotton. An average bale of cotton weighed about five hundred pounds and usually sold for about $50.

It was generally expected that farm children were kept out of school during harvest time. An education didn't seem important to Mama and Daddy. We picked the cotton fields three times before the bulk of it was done, so my sisters and I often missed part of the first semester. In fact, my third grade records show that I was absent eighteen days, and my ninth grade records indicate that I missed twenty-three days. Determined to finish school, I did makeup work and studied hard to catch up. There must be a better way to make a living, I thought, and vowed, "No picking cotton after I graduate."

Late scattered cotton bolls continued to open throughout October and November. We picked those after school. We trotted down each row and grabbed the lone cotton here and there, which earned the phrase *courir les grabots* (running after the bolls). The cotton was packed in burlap sacks, which Daddy sold for about forty cents per hundred pounds, netting him a few dollars.

The sharecropper's barguine specified that Daddy receive no cash until both charge accounts were paid, which left him with barely enough money from his one-third share to compensate him for a year of work or to buy us a few pieces of clothes and winter shoes. The landlord considered Daddy's meager crops a result of his young family helpers and told him to move. It was a losing cycle, repeated every year with no way to get out of the poverty hole.

❖

At the start of eighth grade, when I was fourteen years old, Daddy's deficient work force of three young girls had become fast cotton pickers, and that year we finished picking all our own cotton early and started school on time. Anticipating the new school year, I longed for the treasures of books that challenged my brain, instead of the sharecropper's work that overworked my body.

"Cotton Pickers for Hire, Cash Paid by Day or by Week," said large signs posted at several neighboring farms. By word of mouth Daddy got the news. Just like that, he announced that he had hired himself out, along with Jeanette, Betty, and me. I was angry, but he kept talking.

"This money will buy you new clothes and shoes," he promised.

The more cotton I picked, the more cash I would get, I thought as he went on. I actually believed that by "hiring out" I would earn money for myself. What a treat it would be to buy my own things with my own cash! Maybe being a cotton picker for hire would prove worthwhile. The next night, Mom and Dad hand-stitched patches over the rips and holes of our old picking sacks.

A wagon or a truck arrived at sunrise to pick us up. For a few more weeks, we dragged our sacks and picked cotton all day. Hired pickers were served lunch and icy water on the breaks. Once in a while the boss handed us cold soda pop. My favorite was cream soda. Ah, *c'était bon*, it was good!

There was much competition between me, Jeanette, and Betty. Under the hot sun, I used both hands and picked fast. At the end of each row, I watched intently as the boss weighed my sack on the large, freestanding balance scale, and I peeked over his shoulder at my daily running tab.

The pounds were tallied for each person at the end of the week, and everyone was paid cash on the spot. I don't recall exactly what we were paid. Research with the Louisiana Department of Agriculture and Forestry indicated that hired cotton pickers were generally paid one cent per pound. A few landlords paid up to two cents per pound, according to verbal comments made at one of my area French Table meetings. (French Tables, or Tables Françaises, are informal gatherings of residents, and often a few tourists, speaking conversational French at a local restaurant enjoying *une tasse de café*. The Table

Française at Dwyer's Café on Jefferson Street is more than twenty years strong, and the most prominent one in Lafayette.) The amount of cotton a person picked in one day varied according to their experience, maturity, and speed. It could be as little one hundred pounds, or as much as two or three hundred pounds per day.

Who among us had picked the most cotton?

In an interview with my sisters several years ago, Betty insisted that she was the best picker and averaged about one hundred twenty-five pounds per day. I *absolutely* have no such recollection! My sixteen-year memory believes we each picked ninety, maybe one hundred pounds per day. Certainly, my well-experienced Daddy picked over two hundred. That amounted to about $2.00 a day for him and $0.90 a day for each of his three girls ($2.70 total).

But who got the cash? Contrary to what I had hoped, I never got any. Not even one nickel was put in my tired, dirty hands, nor into my sisters'. What I do remember is that my hard-earned cash was paid to Daddy and stayed with Daddy. A few pieces of clothes and pairs of shoes were bought for us, but whether from our harvested crops or from our picking for hire, I never knew.

⚜

During plowing, planting, and harvest season, it was Daddy's morning routine for him to round up and harness the mules. I recall several disruptive mornings when the mules rebelled. It seemed that the moment Daddy reached out to catch the bridle, the mule jerked his head and ran away. Patiently, Daddy gave it one more try, to no avail. That's when he called in his troupe of girls. He positioned us at strategic places and warned us to stand our ground and shoo the mules back toward the barnyard gate. But I was afraid of them—they were so large and I was so small—so when the mules got near me I, too, ran away.

Amid loud *tonnerre mes chiens* ("thunder of my dogs," a French cursing metaphor) and shaking his head, Daddy waved his hands at us to round up the mules again and yelled, "Allons essayer une autre fois—let's try it once more!"

I recall the frightening morning when Daddy got so mad at Jerry (the instigator) that after he caught him, he grabbed one of Jerry's ears and bit it! You can be sure we all high-tailed it out of the barnyard! Eventually, Daddy settled and harnessed the mules and headed out for the field.

✤

All went smoothly one early October day as Daddy hitched the team to the one-sided blade plow he used to dig sweet potatoes. At the potato patch he plowed a block of rows to be harvested in one day. Daddy positioned and angled his plow on one side of a potato row as he unearthed the clusters of sweet potatoes still attached to the vines but carefully avoided cutting and bruising them.

While Daddy dug up the rest of the rows, I joined my sisters and got to work gathering the potatoes. We each took one row. With my bare hands, I grabbed a cluster of potatoes and twisted off the vines, then brushed off the clumps of moist dirt. I grouped six or seven potatoes together and put them in mounds on top of the row. What a dirty job! Daddy wouldn't buy on credit the gloves needed for this work either. The potatoes dripped a white sticky sap that stuck to my hands and arms and my legs and feet. Dirt crusted in the sap to become black spots. Wherever my hands touched my face, there went another black smudge. I was miserable as dirt and grime got under my fingernails and toenails. It was almost two o'clock before we finished and took a break to eat our dinner.

Later, the sun leaning about forty-five degrees toward the horizon, we returned to the potato rows. We picked up the piles, tossed them into a wooden crate, and dragged it from mound to mound until it was full. When the crate became too heavy for me or my sisters to drag, Daddy moved it.

Shortly before sundown, Daddy hitched the mules to the *traineau*, picked up the crates, and unloaded them on a path between the fields. He stacked them ten crates high and ten crates across. I listened and learned to count in French with Daddy as he took inventory. He counted by tens to one hundred, en français: "dix, vingt, trente, quarante, cinquante, soixante, soixante-dix, quatre-vingt, quatre-vingt-dix, et cent."

At the end of the day, we all looked like a unique band of black-and-white Mardi Gras attendees, *sans masque* and *sans capuchons* (tall, pointed, decorated hats), or maybe like a new breed of upright zoo animals. Finally, we headed home for cleanup. Kerosene was our specialty goo remover. I dipped an old rag in the kerosene pail and hunted down my black spots. I scrubbed them hard. After I was done, my skin was red, sore, and smelly. I took two warm soapy baths, but the kerosene scent lingered.

Occasionally, we got a heavy night rain that prevented us from digging potatoes the next day. I jumped at the chance to escape to school, but once there, I got embarrassed whenever I noticed a black spot that had escaped my scrutiny the night before.

After the harvest, Daddy was allowed to keep a few crates of potatoes for personal use and next year's mother potatoes. He sold the rest of the crates at market and received one-third share of the cash sale.

⚜

I lived for school and the weekend visits at Mom-Mom Doucet's. But I became increasingly self-conscious of our way of life and felt humiliated if someone from school saw me in the wagon en route to my grandparents'!

Another practice that wounded me during my teenage sharecropping years was the way Daddy left on us alone to work in the fields on Fridays afternoons. About 2:30 P.M., Daddy put down his hoe or unlooped his cotton sack, as the case may be, and simply told us he was going fishing. I watched him gaze at *les grands bois* and the beckoning bayou as he told us to carry on with the work until sundown.

"I'm going fishing for you. I'm going to get our supper," he remarked casually as he left. And return with our supper he did. He always came back with plenty, a mess of six to eight sizable yellow spotted or gray catfish. And it wasn't unusual for him to come home with a turtle for a sauce piquante.

Let me make myself clear, my mama's courtbouillon wasn't anything you could find in a restaurant. Not then. Not now! As she would say, "I'll have none of that red tomato gravy that some people call courtbouillon." It was the best, but it would have been even *better* had I also gotten off early.

Show me the cash! But I never saw any. And frequently being left to work while Daddy went fishing didn't feel right to me either, so I dreamed of a better life.

CHAPTER 7

Bayou Man—Outdoor Man

FISHING—HUNTING—FROGGING—TRAPPING

The outdoor life seemed to call the wanderer and the rambler in Daddy and recognized his instinctive connections to the land, the shadowy woods, and the murky bayous. Fishing, hunting, frogging, and trapping, the stuff that he lived for, took place between cultivating and harvesting the crops. Daddy did not consider this work; it was a sport, a standard part of Cajun life. Not only did the sports put fresh meat on the table but also a bit of ready cash.

"Bayou man" was the term that most adequately described Daddy, like the term "mountain man" described a man who lived off of the mountains. When he was not hand-fishing, he was setting out trout lines. He kept on the lookout for turtles: soft shells, loggerheads, or others, and frequently got one. Either way, he usually caught both fish and turtles. But hand-fishing was his specialty.

A bulky man with dark hair, a ruddy complexion, and a well-worn tan cap tipped low on his forehead, he looked every bit the part of a bayou man. In his usual faded blue denim overalls, often minus shirt and socks, his feet in an old pair of shoes, he liked nothing better than to take off on a Friday afternoon and go fishing.

Before starting out, he checked his pockets to make sure that he had his age-old eight-inch yellow multipurpose Case pocketknife. He opened the blades and inspected them to make sure they were razor-sharp by shaving a few strands of hair from his hand. At the barn, he picked up a gunnysack, flipped it over his shoulder, and set off walking through a barely visible path through the woods to the bayou. He strolled along the banks and scouted up and down until he spotted a hollow log peeking out of the bayou, a likely yellow-cat hideout. Taking stock of his surroundings with his sharp fisherman instincts, he rolled his pant legs twice, halfway to his knees. Holding the sack above his head in one hand, Daddy waded quietly into the muddy water and draped his sack across the log. Slowly, carefully, he glided his hand into the log until he sensed the large catfish hiding in the cool shaded waters. His hand felt its way around the outline of the fish's head and mouth. Quickly, tightly, he hooked his thumb and fingers through the fish's gills and grabbed hard as he dragged the catfish out of the log and into the sack, then tied a knot. Carrying the wet jerking sack over his shoulder, Daddy moved down the bayou for other logs to fish, while looking for turtles. He fished until he had enough for supper.

Daddy always got his "catch of the day." Within a few hours, he returned home with his bounty, usually two large yellow spotted catfish plus three or four medium-sized gray ones. Sometimes it was a huge catfish that weighed close to forty-five pounds and a big loggerhead turtle of nearly thirty-five pounds. Setting up outdoors near the porch, Daddy and Mama gutted and cleaned the fish. We sat around them and listened as Daddy recounted his fishing tales. It seemed he was not afraid of anything. "Once," he said, "instead of

Lee Fontenot's catch of the day, a loggerhead
turtle and yellow catfish, circa 1958.

a fish, my hand felt a large snake. But I grabbed that snake tightly below its head, quickly pulled it out of the log, threw that moccasin far away on the banks, and kept right on fishing."

✦

Lee Fontenot holding a yellow spotted catfish, circa 1958.

Mama and Daddy worked quickly to prepare an outdoor cookout of catfish courtbouillon and fried fish. As a rule the cookout was held outdoors, but a few times the courtbouillon was cooked in the kitchen.

Here is how I recollect Mama made it.

Mama's Best Bayou Catfish Courtbouillon

Have on hand three large black pots with wire handles of 6- or 8-quart capacity.

You will need fresh from the bayou 2 large catfish heads and 3 or 4 whole, small to medium catfish, cleaned and dressed.

Salt, cayenne, and black pepper to taste

1/3 cup cooking oil

8 to 10 pods of garlic, minced

1/2 cup minced onions

1 tablespoon tomato sauce in 1/4 cup water

Thicken with 1 tablespoon flour dissolved in 1/2 cup water.
Garnish with 1/3 cup chopped onion tops and parsley.

Mama rubbed the inside of the fish heads with about two teaspoons of minced garlic, as well as cayenne pepper (heavy with the cayenne), black pepper, and salt, then generously sprinkled additional seasoning over the fish. She put the oil in the bottom of the black pot and lined it with the minced garlic and onions, then layered the catfish on top. She mixed the tomato sauce with the water, spooned it around the fish and covered the pot with its tight lid. Mama set the pot upon a bed of hot wood coals and let it simmer for about twenty minutes.

From time to time she lifted the pot by its wire handle and gently rocked it from side to side, basting the catfish. Only once did she check and adjust the seasoning. Five minutes before serving, she added the thickening mixture one teaspoonful at a time into the pockets of gravy and stirred gently to avoid flaking the fish. She replaced the lid for another few minutes, then removed the pot from the coals and garnished it with green onions tops and parsley. Now it was ready to be served with the hot rice she had cooked next to the catfish in the second black pot.

Ah-ah, savor that cooking aroma!

Daddy's Fried Catfish

In the meantime, Daddy filleted the large catfish into thick strips. He seasoned these liberally with salt and cayenne and rolled the fish in homemade cornmeal. He ladled lard into the third black pot to the halfway mark and balanced the pot over the hot coals and open flame until the oil was ready for frying. Daddy dropped the strips into the hot oil and fried these until they were golden brown. The perfect side to the delicious courtbouillon!

Bon appétit!

✦

"Gros Fatty," as Daddy's friends called him, didn't own a vehicle, but his fishing buddies did. Mr. Daigle, whom we called Mr. Polom, and Mr. Picard, whom we called Mr. Uriell, both had trucks. Mr. Polom's mentally disabled son, Deuce, and his younger brother, Moise—nicknamed Tee Joe—completed the fishing party. Once or twice a month they came in their old pickup trucks, loaded with rolls of fishing nets, to pick up Daddy and his bundle of nets. A lively discussion followed to select one of the numerous bayous around Acadia or Saint Landry Parish as their destination. Bayou Queue de Tortue, or Bayou des Cannes? Bayou Mallet or Bayou Nezpique? Finally, the fishing party settled on a bayou. Upon arriving there, the capable and experienced Cajun fishermen unloaded their long heavy nets and set about *seining* the bayou. All day long they cast their nets, and after each catch they moved the nets down a quarter of a mile or so and cast again. Late afternoon, the fishermen loaded their nets and the day's catch and headed home with blue catfish, yellow catfish, gray catfish, garfish, other unidentified fish, and several varieties of turtles, later divided between them. They finished the day with a fish cookout in our backyard with the usual courtbouillon and fried fish. We all feasted with second servings!

After sundown, Daddy untangled the fishing nets and draped them over the fence. The following day, he checked and repaired every rip and tear in his nets with a large needle threaded with fishing twine before he rolled and stored them away.

✦

Rabbits, squirrels, birds, sometimes ducks, and even coons were all fair game for a meal of fresh meat. These were skinned and dressed with a marinade and found their way into pots of rusty brown gravies, jambalayas, or gumbos. During his hunting runs, Daddy also forged around the bushy undergrowth and gathered herbs and roots such as *racine de mamou* (root of mamou plants). Mama used these to make cough syrup, medicinal remedies, and teas.

✤

Frogging was a big part of Daddy's bayou soul. Except for the months of April and May, frog season was open year-round. About once a week at dusk, Daddy gathered his frogging gear in the corner of the kitchen: carbide headlight; grabber device (similar to a hoe with a blade-like spring-device, which grabbed and closed over a frog when thrown); long, pointed frogging stick; pitchfork; gunnysacks; and his knee-high rubber boots. About 10:00 P.M. of the moonless dark night, he strapped the headlight around his head, slipped on his boots, and picked up his gear. On the lookout for bullfrogs, he plodded his way through rice fields, ditches, coulees, or the edges of a bayou.

Daddy was adept at this too, and thirty to forty frogs were a natural result of one night's outing. Considered a delicacy, some went into Mama's sauce piquante. Any extras were sold for cash to local restaurants or friends, all eagerly awaiting a share of the frogs.

Trapping was an additional source of handy cash and called for another venture to the bayou. Minks and nutrias were his quest. Daddy loaded his traps into his ever-ready gunnysack, draped it across his back, and hiked his way to the bayou's water inlets. By sixth sense and experience, he scouted for the most lucrative spots, set his traps, and came home. The next morning, he returned to the traps, removed the snared furry animals, and brought them home in his sack. Daddy skinned the minks and nutria, then scraped and stretched the furs on racks to cure. He sold these to specialized markets for pocket cash.

Lee Fontenot sits on crate, circa 1958.
Note the isolation of the prairie.

I often overheard fragments of arguments between Mama and Daddy. It seemed some of the cash went to buy coffee, sugar, salt, cornmeal . . . but many times some went to buy whiskey, and some was lost playing Bourré.

I never understood the call of the bayou and the dark woods or the wanderer in my Cajun Daddy. Although he frequently left me and my sisters working in the fields, we did enjoy some leisure activities and had fun holidays.

CHAPTER 8

Easter—Leisure—Christmas

POCKING EGGS—THAT OLD YELLOW DOG—
MOM-MOM'S SANTA

My Cajun French sharecropping family worked hard and played hard. Side by side, we harvested the crops, kept the faith, feasted, and made merry holidays.

Ash Wednesday, typically in March, was followed by forty days of Lent. "Eat no meat on Fridays," and "No fais do-dos," were prevalent reminders for us as Catholics to do penance. Some families adopted a "no music at all" rule. Mom-Mom Doucet solemnly reminded me and her other grandchildren to pray the rosary and attend church missions. The public schools also allowed us to attend the Way of the Cross on Fridays. It was indeed a somber time. By the end of Holy

Week, we were ready to lighten up. Good Friday was a holiday at both church and school.

On Good Friday, all spring cultivation and field work halted. Instead, Daddy went fishing. He returned with a big mess of catfish, and we enjoyed an early supper of courtbouillon and fish-fry with relaxed down time. Mama took count of our brown country eggs in anticipation of dyeing them the next day. Saturday morning, Mama fired up the potbellied stove as she gathered the things she used to dye our eggs. We did not have store-bought dye; instead, Mama slowly boiled our eggs in separate pots of water with natural ingredients for different colors.

For rich browns and tans, she cooked the eggs in thick layers of previously used coffee grounds, which she had saved for several weeks. For various shades of green, the eggs were simmered in leaves Daddy had cut from the catalpa tree, or catawba, as we commonly called it. Numerous shades of pink resulted when she boiled the eggs with beets. Carrots colored the boiled eggs orange. Eggs simmered in yellow onion skins and cabbage were pale shades of yellow. Those cooked with red cabbage were various shades of blue-green, and those cooked in red onion peels produced a rusty red color. Sometimes Mama rolled the hot plain boiled eggs in a shallow dish of blue laundry solution for pale blue hues.

I was about ten years old when Mama let me help transfer eggs from one pot to another. The dyed eggs were dried and cooled on an old towel and later put in a padded dishpan. Still, we knew that ours wouldn't compare well to our cousin's tie-dying creations with pieces of colorful fabric. Because Mama didn't sew, we didn't have any scraps.

Egg dying done, Mama made a fig and blackberry pie. Saturday evening, our baths and hair washings were done with great care. Even though we didn't have new clothes, our dresses were freshly washed, starched, and ironed to look our best. All dressed up Sunday morning, bright and early, we were all giggles and full of anticipation

Fontenot children with Mama, circa 1949. Top, left to right: Betty
(about 9 years old), Chère Alice (about 29), Viola (about 11); bottom:
Lester (about 6), Myrtis (about 3), and Jeanette (about 10).

as we climbed into the waiting wagon with our pies and colorful
eggs on our way to Mom-Mom Doucet's Easter feast.

After our dusty gravel road ride, we got to Mom-Mom and
Pop-Pop Doucet's house and disembarked from our wagon, ready
for a fun day with our eleven aunts and uncles and many cousins.
Mom-Mom, beaming and happy, kissed and hugged each of us as
she did the other twenty-five or more family members. Mama's two

younger sisters, Mary Lou, a year older than me, and Laura Lee, a year younger, were eagerly waiting to have an Easter egg hunt.

An hour or so later, the Paquer (Tap) the Egg contest started. A lot of posturing and teasing went on as each person wanted to be declared the champion with the bragging rights. One person held an egg firmly in their fist with only the smaller, pointed top of the egg showing, the second person proceeded to gently tap the tip of their egg against it. The champion was the person who broke the most eggs.

The loud teasing escalated whenever it was discovered that Uncle Mann (Herman) and Uncle Negg (Milton) had tricked us and had used a round or oblong colored rock, or had sneaked in a guinea egg. Both were strictly against the rules, and they were instantly disqualified! The Paquer the Egg fun went on and off all day as different families came and went.

About a dozen broken eggs went into the traditional Easter potato salad. Other sides included sweet peas, *haricot* (snap-beans), carrots, and *chou cru* (raw cabbage or coleslaw), all fresh from the garden. On top of Mom-Mom Doucet's propane stove were large pots of rice dressing, and the oven had garlic-stuffed pork roasts and baked geese. A variety of cakes and pies rounded out the mouth-watering meal, which was served with pitchers of homemade root beer.

It was my family's Cajun tradition that all grownups be served first, starting with the men, next the ladies, and last, the children. We considered it disrespectful for children to eat before the adults. After the big feast, Mama and her six sisters, along with the sisters-in-law, pitched in to clean up the stacks of dirty dishes and the black pots and pans.

The grandchildren were rousted outdoors to play and broke out into groups. We played games such as Ring around the Roses, London Bridge, and Hide and Go Seek, which we called "Hide and Go See." The younger boys played tag, leap frog, or marbles. My older cousins played some version of Hit the Can. They divided into two teams and each person grabbed a long stick or a sturdy branch. A can was placed on a tree stump as home base. Three other bases were outlined, similar to a baseball field. Although improvised at times, the object of the game was to hit the can off the stump with your stick and run to the bases before a player picked it up and tagged you. By sundown, tired, happy, and relaxed, everyone went home. During those years, there were no extra school days off, so Monday was back-to-school for me, and Daddy went back in the fields to plow and do the spring planting.

✤

We had some leisure days during the early summer months before we started picking cotton and digging sweet potatoes. Then, after we harvested the crops, we had a long leisurely period during winter.

My sisters and I spent time sitting on the porch or under a tree, leafing through the Alden's catalog. I daydreamed about pretty clothes and yearned for matching shoes. Other times, I watched the clouds make fascinating formations and named them. While stargazing, I listened to crickets and chirpy things create a harmony of their own. After dark, I loved the endearing pastime of chasing and catching fireflies. I kept two or three of them under a clear canning jar on a table near our bed and watched them blink until I was lulled to sleep.

✤

These *en français, s'il vous plaît* (in French, if you please) games stand out as my favorites. I learned them from my Cajun French Mom-Mom Doucet, and my own soul always felt that the oral French language was more fun and descriptive than the English language.

Cache, Cache Bien la Bague (Hide, Hide Well the Ring) was a game played indoors or outdoors, either sitting or standing in a circle, with all hands clasped in the "praying position." The "It" person stood inside the circle hiding a flat button or a butterbean in their clasped hands and pretended it was a "magic ring." The object of the game was for the "It" person to stand inside the circle and go from hand to hand, pretending to transfer the magic ring into someone's hands while chanting, "cache, cache bien la bague" over and over again. "It" made false pretenses and gestures to mislead who received the "magic ring." After "It" dropped the ring into a pair of hands, he or she called upon a player to guess who had it. If the selected player guessed the wrong person, then the wrong person took the next guess and continued until someone guessed correctly. That person became "It" and the game started over. The rhythmic chants of "cache, cache bien la bague" about the magic ring added zing to the game.

Le Petit Oiseau Vole (The Little Bird Flies): Akin to Simon Says, all players placed their index finger on the surface of the table or on the floor, and a caller was appointed. The caller began the game by calling, "Le petit oiseau vole" and raised his or her index finger high. Since birds can fly, all players quickly raised their fingers then quickly put them down, and waited for the next call. A player who failed to raise their finger promptly was out. The caller kept calling creatures that did fly, then suddenly called something that could not fly to fool a player into raising their hand. When one did, that person was out, and the game continued until only one player remained, the winner.

For example, the caller might say, "l'oiseau vole," "le maringouin (mosquito) vole," "la cigale (cicada) vole," "la tasse (cup) vole." "No, la tasse vole pas"—the cup does not fly! If you raised your finger, you were out.

Of course, there were the timeless games of hopscotch and jump rope and card games such as *bataille* (battle) or matching suits.

I learned this English game from a fifth grade friend. The game was called "Pass the Shoe." All players took off one shoe and dropped it in a corner and kept the other one in their hand. Everyone sat on the floor in a circle, placed their shoe in front of them, and started singing, "I'm gonna pass this shoe from me to you, to you, I'm gonna pass this shoe, and do just like I do." In rhythm, each person passed their shoe to their right. On the first "do" everyone kept the shoe they had in their hand and tapped it on the floor to their right. On the word "like," the same shoe was tapped to the left. On the second "do," everyone passed the shoe to the player on their right, and the game continued. The object of the game was to catch someone without a "shoe" on the second "do." That person was out. The last one to have a shoe in their hand was declared the winner. It was silly, fun, and the more the merrier. Locating your own shoe in the corner after the game proved even more comical!

✤

Daddy was a great storyteller. On some dark nights, in the dim light of a smoky kerosene lamp, we were treated to his stories en français! This often happened unanticipated when we were playing on the floor near him. Daddy loudly cleared his throat to get our attention and worked up his story. The following stories are a few that I remember to this day.

Once upon a time a man went to a veillée. Content and whistling under his breath, he was driving his buggy back home down an isolated lane through the big woods. Suddenly, *la bétaille loup-garou* (werewolf beast) materialized in the road in front of him. The frightened horse spooked, reared his head, and took off running. The startled and scared man lost control of the reins and his horse. The horse galloped wildly, pulling the buggy and the rider through *les grands bois*. A few miles later, in total disbelief and shaken to the core, the man regained control and nervously made his way back home. He breathlessly told his family and friends all about his mysterious and terrifying encounter with *la bétaille loup-garou*! The man's tale was often repeated and exaggerated, and Daddy did it well.

"This is a true hunting story," my father began one night in his slow-drawled Cajun French. "Years ago, when we were young men, me and three of my brothers went hunting deep in the tall thick woods near our place in the Pitreville community of Acadia Parish. All at once, we found ourselves standing in the middle of a clearing of bright sunlight without any trace of trees or bushes near us. Our eyes squinted to adjust to the brightness after being in the dark shade for hours. Puzzled, we looked around and walked some, when out of nowhere there appeared an old red brick mound. Baffled and curious, we inspected it closely. Slowly, it dawned on us that we had found the long ago rumored hidden Civil War treasure!"

"After a discussion," said Daddy, "we walked back to a group of trees and used our knives and notched three or four trees to mark the location. We hurried home, grabbed shovels, and quickly made our way back to the red brick mound. But everything had disappeared! We searched for hours, and although the woods were very familiar, as we regularly hunted there, no clearing was found, not one marked tree, not even one small hill, was evident anywhere."

Daddy went on to tell us that he and his brothers went back many times and looked for the alleged Civil War treasure. They never found any traces of the notched trees or the mysterious brick mound. The Civil War treasure story lingers in my soul. Sometimes, I still hear Daddy tell the story.

The funniest stories Daddy told us were about Brer Rabbit and the Tar Baby. His elaborate gestures of sparring with an imaginary puppet kept us laughing wildly as he added new antics and improvised the story each time. Those were the days of storytelling en français. Like the old games, it was truly a unique experience.

⚜

Candy-making became part of my leisure activities as an early teenager. I had watched Mama make pralines with eggs, sugar, and cream on the three-burner kerosene stove. One early afternoon, Mom and Dad went for a *promenade* (visit) to the neighbors', and I decided to make candy. Jeanette and Betty watched my first attempt, which turned out brittle and grainy. I threw it away and started over. By instinct, I adjusted the sugar and cream. To my surprise and satisfaction, this time it came out good. With great pride I dropped the pralines by tablespoon full onto an old cake pan and set it out on the porch to cool. Meanwhile, my sisters and I cleaned up the kitchen.

Lee Fontenot and Myrtis with the old yellow dog in front of our sharecropper house. Pitreville, Acadia Parish, circa 1947.

An hour or so later we went on the porch to eat our pralines, but lo and behold, we caught our old yellow dog, Rex, happily licking his chops! Not one piece was left. We were furious! We scolded and chased that old yellow dog until he hid in a hole under the house. He peeked out at us with his hang-dog look and droopy eyes. He knew he had done wrong! For days my sisters reproached me for putting my pralines on the porch. And for months, I rebuked that old yellow dog, Rex.

I didn't give up, though. Each time Mama and Daddy left for a visit, I tried something new. Most times we had peanuts and sugarcane syrup in stock, either bought or traded with the neighbors. Particularly in winter, I roasted peanuts in the shells in the black stove oven. Other times, I roasted the fresh-shelled peanuts in a black skillet stove-top. While the peanuts were still warm, I went outside and poured the peanuts from one dishpan into another to let the breeze fan away the skins. With practice I learned to make peanut brittle and chewy peanut-syrup bars. One day, quite by accident, I made cane syrup taffy.

I put the sugar cane syrup to boil and added a bit of PET milk. I cooked and stirred and cooked some more. But it stayed in the soft ball stage. Frustrated, I beat the mixture by hand, hoping it would become firm. Not to be. It remained soft and gummy! I held the soft ball between my fingertips and starting pulling. It got stringy and thinner. In desperation, I gave some to my sisters. Within minutes, they too had syrup strings on their hands, arms, and in their hair. Ultimately, we erupted into fits of laughter and giggles and had fun with it. Finally, I threw away the whole mess, and we quickly washed and cleaned up everything before Mom and Dad came home. Although there were other episodes in the kitchen, these are the ones that never fail to make me chuckle.

⚜

December marked the end of sharecropping work!

Christmas—revered and special—was a two-day, all-night big family affair at Mom-Mom Doucet's. It was a time for Cajun music and joie de vivre. There would even be a Christmas tree!

At our house, Christmas Eve morning was Mama's cake-making time. The potbellied stove all fired up, she arranged on her table flour, sugar, homemade butter, baking powder, vanilla, and a pan of fresh brown country eggs. Mixing bowls, spoons, sauce pans, and cake pans were likewise handy.

From scratch and by memory, Mama sifted enough flour with pinches of baking powder to make two three-layered cakes. She creamed the butter and sugar, added eggs and some milk, and stirred and mixed. Daddy's strong arms beat the batter until it was light and fluffy, then poured it in the pans. Mama made two saucepans of vanilla pudding, then added drained crushed pineapple to one and shredded coconut to the other. She spread the pudding between the layers of warm cake.

Daddy took charge of making the meringue icing. He put his large pottery bowl on an old wooden table outside under a tree and beat the egg whites until fluffy. He slowly added the sugar and a tad of vanilla, and kept beating until the meringue was high and stiff. Mama helped Daddy ice the cakes. Impatiently, we all gathered around to scrape the bowls and lick the spoons. By 3:00 P.M. on Christmas Eve, we were all spruced up and ready to go to Mom-Mom Doucet's. Daddy hitched the wagon, which was loaded with the cakes and our Christmas dress clothes. Mama bundled us in quilts and blankets, and off we went for our Veillée de Christmas.

Upon arriving, we were joyfully greeted by Mom-Mom and Mama's many brothers and sisters: Aunt Minnie, Aunt Rena, Aunt Rita, Uncle Willis, Uncle Leonce, and Uncle Wilson; the unmarried uncles, Herman and Milton; Mama's younger sisters, Aunts Mary Lou and Laura Lee; and all our cousins.

And on top of that, Mom-Mom had put up a Christmas tree! In the corner of the living room near a double wide window, the tall pine tree was decorated with tassels and shining red, silver, and gold ropes. Dozens of colorful ornaments dangled all over it.

The children played outside and enjoyed popcorn balls and tea cakes. At dusk, and throughout the evening, our uncles lit many boxes of sparklers and helped us pop endless packs of firecrackers. About 10:00 P.M. they lit up an assortment of brilliant fireworks that dazzled us.

In the kitchen, Mom-Mom and her entourage of daughters and daughters-in-law were hard at work making a huge Christmas Eve chicken and sausage gumbo to eat after Midnight Mass. (Catholics did not eat meat on Christmas Eve). Three of them swiftly chopped heaps of onions, garlic, and peppers, while Mom-Mom made a brown roux in her favorite black iron skillet. Others cooked several pots of rice and made potato salad.

Meanwhile, in the large living-dining room, the men played Cajun music, sang old French ballads, and had their toddies. Daddy first, then Uncle Wilson, played the accordion. Someone produced a fiddle. Another played his harmonica. For rhythm and timing, Mama and her sisters took turns clapping big spoons together, or rubbed a flattened fork on the washboard. It was fun to catch my aunts joyfully dancing a spontaneous jig!

The merriment stopped promptly at 11:00 P.M. Mom-Mom was firm that. The buggies, wagons, and horses were hitched up, and most adults went to Midnight Mass.

Back from Mass, the group of merrymakers, now sober and hungry, scrambled for a heaping bowl of steaming gumbo served over hot rice with a side of potato salad.

After the kitchen cleanup, things quieted down. Giggling and whispering, the children and teenagers went to bed wherever there was room, in rockers, on padded benches, or shared beds, even on quilts on the floor. It was hard to go to sleep as we impatiently waited for Santa Claus.

I was barely slumbering when I was awakened by a noisy ruckus on the porch that was followed by a loud door slam. I saw a shadow cross the windows as I scrambled to the floor to check it out, and I heard someone talking.

"Ah ha, could it be Santa Claus?" questioned Uncle Mann.

"Yes, it must be," someone else replied.

"Look! What's that?" I heard, as every grownup got into the act.

"Check out the Christmas tree," Aunt Rita called out.

I saw lots of colorful wrapped presents piled under the tree! Mom-Mom gave a gift to each grandchild and to her four unmarried children. For the smaller girls, it was tea sets and a baby doll; for teenage girls, it was Pond's face cream. Each child had a bag of fruit, candy, and gum—rare at our house. My unmarried uncles received a carton of Lucky Strike cigarettes, a luxury as they typically hand-rolled their own. As we opened our presents, we saw Santa Claus (i.e., Uncle Leonce, nicknamed "Yonce") sneaking around the corner of the house on his way to the neighbors'.

Pop-Pop Doucet was the quiet one, the one who observed it all as he smoked his cigarette. And Mom-Mom? Well, she kept smiling as she patted our shoulders and moved from one grandchild to the next and beamed with happiness and pride at everyone! I always felt that Mom-Mom loved me dearly.

On Christmas Day there was a feast fit for a king. Mom-Mom and her helpers cooked many things. There was stuffed pork roast, baked turkey, and a roasted goose. She had spicy sausages, smoked stuffed *pounce*, rice dressing, potato salad, coleslaw, fruited Jell-O, and an assortment of cakes and pies. There was root beer and sweetened watered-down red wine punch. Even the kids were given a taste of it.

For two days we ate, played, and had a grand Santa veillée! Soon enough, late Christmas Day, everyone packed and left for home.

However, one Christmas celebration didn't turn out so well for me.

I remember this particular Christmas morning, when I was four or five years old. I woke up at Mom-Mom's with a high fever and a hacking cough. Daddy rushed to get us back home. Struggling against the cold blowing wind and a misty rain, he wrapped me and my sisters in heavy blankets and quilts and settled us in the wagon. Hurrying the mules to a fast trot, we headed home.

I had the measles, and my sisters caught it, too. There we were—all together in our homemade baby bed, coughing and feverish, our little bodies covered with welts of red rash. Mama treated us with homemade cough syrup, Vicks salve, aspirin, and cooling sponge baths. For days, she had no rest.

With that lone exception, Christmas veillée at Mom-Mom and Pop-Pop Doucet's is still one of my most treasured childhood memories.

CHAPTER 9

Waiting for the Cab

CAJUN COURTSHIP: HIGH SCHOOL DANCE,
NOT SO, BUT CAJUN DANCE, LET'S GO!

Shy and timid, I often lived in my head. In my junior year, I hoped to be invited to a high school dance. Wishful thinking, I knew, but there it was. I was like any other teenager—clothes, shoes, and boys were important!

In chapter 5, I stated that my sisters and I had grown taller and stronger, and we worked more acres. A bigger harvest of cotton netted Daddy more money. Mama said we had extra cash and that Daddy would take us shopping. She even said I could choose my own clothes! This was new; Mama and Daddy had always bought all our things.

From my endless captivation with mail order catalogues, I had formed my own ideas on how to dress attractively. Skirts and blouses offered more variety. My home economics sewing classes provided valuable tips to alter clothes. A tuck at the waist, pinned inside with a safety-pin, and concealed with a contrasting belt, added style and made the clothes fit me better.

Eager for my first shopping trip, I climbed in the wagon with the whole family as Daddy drove us to Mr. Oscar Guidry's store near Church Point. My eyes widened with surprise at the rows and rows of assorted merchandise. Mama firmly guided me down the over-sized room to the discounted bins of bras and undies, but not before I had a glance at the pretty clothes displayed at the entrance.

Following a long aisle, we stopped at a clothes rack where I found two blouses and one skirt to match, and one wide black patent leather belt to add interest and extend my outfits. Mama got two new dresses, Daddy and Lester got new overalls and shirts, and my sisters got several pieces of school clothing. I used the word "got" as we, the children, never had money to buy things. Each of us got a new pair of shoes, and for the first time, bras for the girls. I wanted to explore the store, but Mama did not let us linger. I was upset that the shopping ended so quickly.

✤

Sitting on the steps of the shaded worn-out porch, I was flipping the pages of the Alden's catalogue when a cute pair of sandals caught my eye. I stared a long time at the red, low-wedge sandals trimmed in white. I turned to the next page but went right back. I fell in love with them and daydreamed that I had a pair! Finally, I could stand it no more.

I jumped up, went to the kitchen, and pointed to the sandals on the page. I gushed out all in one breath, "Mama, I just love these red sandals, may I please order them?"

She shrugged as she replied, "You have to ask your dad."

Always a little fearful of him, I retreated and waited for the next day. Finally, I gathered up my courage and nervously approached him.

"Please, Daddy, may I order myself this pair of red and white sandals?" I asked, showing him the picture. He looked at it briefly, then turned his head away.

"No, we don't have money for that," was his gruff, dismissive reply.

I flinched inside, but knew that it was useless for me to say more. I crumpled the page, moved away, and squeezed my eyes tight to stop the tears. The next day I overheard Mama and Daddy arguing. He had lost our money gambling and had none for my sandals. It was a bitter pill to swallow.

However, children are resilient and I was soon contemplating another thought.

After the field work was over, I decided that I would approach Mama with my idea of going Cajun dancing. At the time we were living on Prudhomme road in the Pitreville community of Acadia Parish, located about fifteen miles east of Eunice. I asked Mama if I could go dancing, but she pretended not to hear. By then, I was almost sixteen years old, Jeanette close to fifteen, and Betty fourteen. We had learned to dance in the kitchen while Daddy jammed on his Cajun accordion on Saturday mornings, and later that day we danced a jitterbug or two during the "Happy Fats" radio program.

Following the jam, Daddy customarily shaved, dressed, and hitch-hiked a ride to Nick's Bar in Eunice to play cards. Leaving Nick's at nightfall, Daddy walked a few miles along the old Crowley Road Highway 26 (now Highway 13) to Club 26, where he played another round of cards in the back room while the Cajun dances were going on. After it was over, he took a cab home.

Mama didn't say too much about us going to the dances, but I could tell she hated being left with her three teenage daughters and two younger kids on Saturday nights.

A few weeks later I spoke to her again. "Mama, could you please ask Daddy to take us dancing to Club 26? You could visit with friends, and at the same time make new ones." I feverishly hoped she would try.

This time she did take our case to Daddy. At first he wouldn't hear any of it. However, in time he agreed to Mama's suggestion that after he hitchhiked to Eunice on Saturdays, he would send a cab about 7:00 P.M.to fetch us—that is, Mama, me, Jeanette, Betty, Lester, and little sister Myrtis—to Club 26.

And so began our waiting for the cab.

Anticipation was high on Saturday afternoons. Hustling and giggling as the old battery radio played on, we took turns bathing in the number-three size washtub. We washed our hair and rolled it on Seaport Coffee tie-wraps (as was the style). Smiling and humming a tune, we dressed up and put on makeup. It was the first time we were going dancing! Mama, too, was in on the fun and enjoyed getting herself, Lester, and Myrtis spruced up for a night out. In those days, dances were chaperoned by the whole family.

We watched and waited! Sometimes, Daddy kept his word and a cab arrived for us about 7:00 P.M., and the fun and dancing was on at Club 26. Other times, Daddy drank too much and forgot. Our three pair of eyes watched through the window panes, our fingers crossed, hoping and waiting for the cab. Hours later, kneeling on the floor, I still hoped to see the cab's headlights come down the country road. Finally, past 10:00 P.M., I gave up. With teardrops spotting my cheeks, I crawled in bed, feeling discouraged and betrayed.

The following Saturday, we did it all over again, believing and waiting for the cab. It was almost like gambling—maybe we'd get lucky tonight, and sometimes we were.

One particular Saturday night at Club 26, my sisters and I became friendly with Ernest Courville, Floyd Smith, and L.J. Thibodeaux. It turned out that Ernest and Floyd were first cousins, and L.J. was their second cousin. We began hanging out. Although I preferred to dance, as did my sisters, the guys hung out at the jukebox and smoked. Even so, there was an undeniable attraction between me and Ernest and between Betty and Floyd. It wasn't long before Ernest asked me if he could come visiting at home on Sunday afternoons.

"Courting" was the Cajun cultural time-honored tradition of calling upon and visiting a young lady at home while she was chaperoned. That was acceptable to Daddy, but les américains' way of "dating" he held in contempt.

Two rockers, often used in Cajun courting. LARC Acadian Village.

It turned out to be "double courting," as Ernest and Floyd both came. They didn't mind the courting ways since the guys, like me and Betty, spoke French first and were raised in the Cajun culture. After all, they didn't have much spending money to take us out on dates!

Le parloir, our small spare room with bare wood floors, lacked a sofa. It was sparsely furnished with two pairs of brown, scratched, wooden rockers, side by side. Not only was Mama in the adjoining room with the door ajar, Jeanette and Lester were constantly barging in. Eight-year-old Myrtis interrupted us too—she came in to get her Bit-o-Honey or other such candy bars that Ernest and Floyd brought for her. The chaperoned courting was not conducive to romance, but I enjoyed having my own special friend.

I was seventeen when Ernest and I started going steady. Although Betty was sixteen, she and Floyd started going steady during the same time. Daddy agreed that the guys could bring Mama and the rest of us out on Saturday nights to Club 26. Thankfully, there was no more waiting for the cab.

It was the end of my junior year, and I had a boyfriend that I could count on. I considered myself almost out of the cotton fields! Next year I would graduate and say goodbye to sharecropping.

CHAPTER 10

High School Distress— Graduation—Marriage

CAJUN GIRL MARRIES CAJUN BOY—NEW BEGINNINGS

"Oh, no, we're moving!" groaned my teenage soul.

Daddy dropped the bomb the first week of December 1953, my junior year at Church Point High. Another landlord had turned us out, a familiar pattern since first grade. This time, the move was out of Acadia Parish and into Saint Landry Parish, a different school district almost forty miles from Pitreville. I was furious! With my high GPA, I was in line for class valedictorian, and I wanted that honor. "This is so unfair," I moaned to my sisters and Mama. Silently, I vowed, "One day I will own my own home where no one can make me move." Venting didn't change a thing, and my school records are noted "dropped, transcript sent to Eunice High December 10, 1953."

Once more, we move down a rutted lane to another small run-down farmhouse, this one with a screened-in porch. The place was situated on the old Chataignier Road in Saint Landry Parish, almost five miles north of Highway 190 and the Cedric Fruge's store, nearly fifteen miles east of Eunice.

Several days later, five Fontenot children—Viola, Jeanette, Betty, Lester, and Myrtis—boarded a Saint Landry Parish school bus and checked in at new schools in Eunice, Louisiana.

I was dismayed when I learned that Eunice High was part of an advanced school district that was six weeks ahead of Church Point High. While I quickly caught up in the other subjects, I struggled with the missed equations in geometry. I stayed in at recess for extra help and buried myself in geometry at night, but my grade dropped from A to C my first semester at Eunice High. I came back strong in the next one and brought the geometry grade back to an A, but the damage to my GPA was done.

I pressed forward both at school and at home.

I wanted my own bed! I had asked Mama once before, but my plea went unanswered. I tried again. "Mama," I pleaded, "me, Jeanette, and Betty are all grown up, and Myrtis is six years old, and we're all sleeping together! It's so hot and crowded with four in the bed. Please, as the oldest, can I get my own bed?"

A few weeks later, something finally happened. I got home from school, and there it was, a single-sized cot all set up on the screened porch! She did not say who gave it to me, and I did not ask. And for the first time in my life, I had my very own bed, in my very own room!

My former Church Point rural friends, like me, didn't go to school functions. However, most of my new friends at Eunice High lived in town and did participate in after-school activities. They even went out on dates! I was pretty good at basketball and was selected for the team. But regrettably, Daddy refused to allow my friends to come pick me up for practice. I let it go, though I begrudged him for keeping me from playing basketball.

Betty didn't like the new school and did poorly in math, so Mama subtly cajoled her into quitting school by saying she needed help with housekeeping. That didn't sound right to me because Jeanette and I did the laundry and ironing on Saturdays. Daddy didn't object either as he was often not home. I tried to dissuade my sister, but she dropped out of school early in the ninth grade. Perhaps it had something to do with her growing affections for Floyd.

Romance was underway and hormones fluctuated and flickered while Ernest and Floyd continued to come courting. The Saturday night dances were still going on, but so was school.

⚜

Did I misunderstand the title? Or did I get the assignment wrong? "Read the book *Derby Dick*, and then write a book report." That is what I had understood my literature teacher to assign as a catch-up project during my third week of school. I searched every shelf and every card catalogue at the school library for that book to no avail.

The next day, standing close to my teacher, I shyly told her that I couldn't find the book *Derby Dick* anywhere in the library.

"The book's title is *Moby Dick*, not *Derby Dick*," my teacher quietly replied.

Humiliation set in, and my face flushed scarlet red as the whole class erupted into uncontrollable laughter. I didn't understand what was so funny. The names sounded alike. It was then that someone came up to me and explained that "derby" referred to horse races in Kentucky, and "Moby Dick" was the name of a huge whale in a novel.

Now, how was a Cajun sharecropping girl supposed to know about such things?

Needless to say, horses and whales are worlds apart. I read that boring book and made an A on the report. However, the nickname "Derby Dick" stuck to me as my new classmates continued to tease me, especially the boys.

A few months after the "Derby Dick" episode, another occurrence embarrassed and rattled me. I was leaving my history classroom for the next class when, without any warning, I fainted and crumpled to the floor right outside the door. Next thing I knew, I felt someone sponge my face with a cold towel to revive me.

Squinting, I tried to focus as two teachers helped me up. Standing steady, but ashamed, I assured them that I was alright. Nevertheless, a teacher accompanied me to the home economics room for rest and observation. Upon learning that I had skipped breakfast (dry cornbread since the milk was sour), she fixed me hot tea and toast.

Feeling refreshed from the tea break, I was allowed to resume classes. I never spoke about or acknowledged this humbling incident again. Thereafter, I always ate something each morning before going to school.

⚜

The cherry bomb injury happened shortly before Christmas of my senior year.

Sitting in a circle, basking in warm sunshine on the front campus of Eunice High, me and several girlfriends were chatting while we waited for the second-shift school bus. Impromptu, three of us decided to go buy snacks a few yards away at the corner grocery store.

Since Ernest and I were going steady, he gave me twenty-five cents a week for treats. At that time the cost of a candy bar was five cents, so my twenty-five cents lasted all week. That day I bought a Zero, my favorite candy bar, and my two friends bought bags of chips.

We were walking back three abreast (me in the middle) on the sidewalk, when I suddenly heard, *bang-bang, pop-pop*!

Startled, I looked up and saw two brothers and their friend approaching us. Jostling and laughing, they were lighting firecrackers and throwing small cherry bombs on the sidewalk to scare us.

A fiery sensation spread slowly down my left knee to my ankle as I sagged to the ground and clutched my leg, trying to determine the cause. I stared in disbelief at the dark red blood oozing from a deep round gash. A cherry bomb had bounced up from the sidewalk and exploded on my leg, shredding the flesh almost to the bone!

Minutes later, the duty teacher rushed to see about me and applied first aid to my aching, bleeding leg. The fireworks were quickly confiscated, and the boys were immediately ushered to the principal's office for questioning.

Later, the teacher drove me home and explained the accident to my parents. Mama and Daddy listened, said "merci" to her for taking care of me, and that was the end of it. Fortunately, the crop harvesting was finished and I was not needed in the fields.

A very angry principal called an assembly the next morning and relayed the accident and injury to my leg. Heatedly, he reiterated a long list of dangers associated with having fireworks at school and emphasized that there would be strict punishment for any further infractions of the rules.

Those brothers were always in some kind of mischief. Their parents, well-to-do rice farmers and our distant neighbors, were notified. In fact, the boys rode the same bus as I did. Although fireworks were strictly forbidden at school, they had sneaked some in anyway.

Every day, my leg wound needed to be cleaned and dressed, and I remained on crutches for almost six weeks. To make amends for their misdeeds, the brothers were ordered to assist me with the awkward, painful climb to my second-floor classes until my leg healed. A dime-sized hole and scar remained on my leg for almost ten years.

After the cotton and sweet potatoes were harvested my senior year, and shortly before my eighteenth birthday, Daddy drove me and my sisters in the wagon to shop at Ardoin's pricey department store in Eunice. Totally different from the Oscar Guidry experience, I was allowed to pick out several skirts and blouses, plus I helped choose a lovely cashmere-feel mid-length purple coat for myself. And I got my first pair of stylish black high-heeled pumps!

Bartering was a big deal in the Cajun custom, as this was before the mode of sale items. En français, Daddy kept up what seemed like an endless bartering dialogue "for cash" until all parties agreed to an acceptable cash price and my precious things were wrapped to go. Back home, I paraded all afternoon in the new pumps and soft royal purple coat and contemplated the last few months to graduation.

✤

Significant feelings (felt like love) escalated between me and Ernest, and we talked marriage. Ernest had a service station attendant job and had a flair for playing the guitar, both Cajun and country music. I knew of only two ways out of the cotton fields. One was a suitable Cajun marriage, and the other one was to go to college (which was questionable). I chose marriage, the easy way out.

I accepted an engagement ring from Ernest on my eighteenth birthday on January 7, 1955. When news of my engagement reached my English and home economics teachers, both called me aside several times for a conference. They pointed out that with my good grades, I should go to college, not get married. I explained that I had no means of getting to college, that Daddy did not even own a car. Furthermore, I knew that marriage was the only acceptable and expected lifestyle for a Cajun girl that Daddy and Mama would approve.

During the last months of school, the two teachers even arranged for me to live with a college professor where I could babysit her children while attending Louisiana State University in Baton Rouge. So I sounded Daddy out about that arrangement. I didn't get very far. He flat-out vetoed it. Such things were frowned upon, almost a dishonor in the Cajun culture. "It is wrong to live with les américains étrangers," American strangers, he muttered several times. I didn't have it in me to rebel or disobey, though I was now eighteen years old.

The distress of adjusting to a new school, "Derby Dick," fainting, and a cherry bomb gash on my leg took its toll. Getting married felt okay, and I went on with my plans for a June wedding.

Viola Fontenot. Eunice High School
graduation, May 1955.

A picnic and swimming trip all the way to Lake Arthur, Louisiana, was our senior class trip. I thought that was too far away! This time Daddy said "yes" to the trip and permitted my friends to pick me up. I saw their disbelieving looks at the isolated dirt lane, and the small boxlike farmhouse with the kerosene stove, bare floors, and my cot, but they were kind enough not to make any comments. The outing went well, but I was too shy to fit in, remained aloof all day, and was happy to go home.

I graduated in May 1955 with honors, fifth in my class, and received a four-year scholarship to Louisiana State University in Baton Rouge. I was very proud of that accomplishment and hoped to use it later. Although I embraced my culture and felt blessed to be bilingual, I didn't want to live and work on a sharecropping farm.

Cajun girl marries Cajun boy—I, Viola Fontenot, married Ernest Courville on Sunday, June 12, 1955, with a proper Catholic wedding

Viola Fontenot. Eunice High School graduation, May 1955.

Cajun girl marries Cajun boy. Wedding of Ernest Courville and Viola Fontenot, June 1955.

Cajun backyard wedding reception. Left to right: Nita Courville, Ernest Courville, Viola Fontenot Courville, Alice Doucet Fontenot. Lee and Alice Fontenot's home, old Chataignier Road, Saint Landry Parish, Louisiana, June 1955.

at 1:00 P.M. in Saint Edward's Church, Richard, Louisiana. During those years, Sunday afternoon was the norm for a wedding. My wedding dress was second-hand, and, as was the custom, the bridal bouquet was made with kleenex tissues rather than fresh flowers. Ernest and I and our wedding attendants drove to Eunice for pictures. Mr. and Mrs. Ernest Courville, newlyweds, drove to Mama and Daddy's house on the old Chataignier Road and joined our family, friends, and guests for a backyard Cajun wedding reception. As bride and groom, we cut the wedding cake and celebrated with a variety of homemade cakes served with Mogen David wine punch for the adults and lemonade for the children. There were few wedding presents, but Mama and Daddy gave me a yellow, blue, and green set of mixing bowls. (Years later, one got broken, but I still have two.) A traditional Cajun wedding dance was held at Club 26 on old Crowley Road.

That night, with only our clothes, a few boxes of dishes, and his guitar, Ernest and I moved in temporarily with his sister and brother-in-law, who lived in the Eunice city limits. A few weeks later we rented our own little place about three blocks from them, and I began a new phase in my life.

At last, my sharecropping days were over.

Epilogue

Sharecropping was a hard life, but working side by side with my parents instilled in me a good honest work ethic and resilient character traits that helped me to live a fulfilling life.

Lee and Alice Fontenot continued farming until my brother went to work in the oilfields. Drifting from one prairie house to another near a bayou, Daddy worked at odd jobs, trapped for a living, until his death in a car accident in October of 1966. He was fifty-four years old, and Mama was forty-eight.

Following Daddy's death, Mama never returned to the old place. She and my sister, Myrtis, stayed with me and Ernest. I took care of Mama's paperwork and three weeks later was able to get them into a low-income living complex in Eunice. Myrtis got married the following year, and Mama cooked in restaurants until she remarried in September of 1972. In 1974 her second husband died, and Mama lived by herself in her own house for ten years. Due to a stretch of thyroid cancer, she moved into a nursing home in 2001 and lived there until her death in 2003 at age eighty-three.

While my marriage to Ernest in 1955 got me out of the cotton fields, I soon learned that married life was no picnic. But to my deep satisfaction, this Cajun girl and Cajun boy kept French as our first language.

We set up housekeeping in a three-room run-down house in the Eunice city limits. Our kitchen had an apartment-size refrigerator and stove. An old iron bed with a moss mattress, together with a few stacked cardboard boxes for shelves, took up most of our bedroom. But we had the luxury of a bathroom with hot running water!

Three months into my marriage I took a job as a sales clerk job at the upscale Weill's Department Store. Ernest used his old truck for his service station job, and I walked about a mile to mine. I was proud to be working, and it was an easy walk! Even though there were serious signs of a troubled marriage within the first four months, I felt sure we could overcome them.

Six months later, I was promoted to cashier at Weill's and even bought myself a few pretty dresses with matching shoes! The following year, 1956, I landed a new job as loan clerk and cashier with American Finance. Ernest too got a new and better job as a dragline operator and cement finisher with a Eunice concrete business that lasted more than fifteen years. In March of 1957 I was happy to move into a nice furnished duplex on Saint Joseph Street in Eunice where our daughter was born on October 11, 1957.

But Ernest was restless and hated living in town! In 1958 the Cajun girl and the Cajun boy moved back to the country. We rented a small house five miles east of Eunice's Highway 190, down a country gravel road from Shuff's Truck Stop. Ernest promised me that he intended to buy us our own place.

One year later, in 1959, he kept his word and bought a quarter-acre country tract from a rice farmer. The lot was located across the road from our rented house. Six weeks later, Ernest acquired an old house from an acquaintance in exchange for labor he had done. He had the four-room house moved onto our lot at Route 1, Box 175J, Eunice, Louisiana. Finally, we were bona fide home owners, and no one could make us move! Later that year, our second child was born on August 25, 1959; our third was born on March 11, 1963.

My guitar-playing husband was a natural-born carpenter and jack of all trades. Over the years, Ernest renovated and updated our country house into a nice one-and-one-half-story home with three bedrooms and three baths.

I was a stay-at-home mom and worked part-time while raising our first three kids, Faye, Marty, and Eric. With only one car, I took them with us as I drove Ernest to work by 7:00 A.M. and returned home. On my work days, with the help of my next-door babysitter, I dressed for work and was at my job by 8:00 A.M. We repeated the shift in the afternoons until we bought me a used car. After the kids started school, the school bus picked them up before I left for work. Ernest was home by 4:00 P.M. when the bus dropped them off. Our fourth child, Marleen, was born on November 1, 1970.

Throughout our marriage, from 1959 to 1982, Cajun music was a fun part of our lives. Ernest came from a family of Cajun musicians and was friends with fiddlers and guitar players, including the young Acadian accordion builder and player, Marc Savoy. The Saturday night or Sunday afternoon jams were held at our house during our children's preschool and elementary years, and I often cooked a gumbo. Later, the jams were held at a neighbor's outdoor kitchen. The men played Cajun music while the women socialized, had fun, sometimes sang along, and cooked a large pot of gumbo or a sauce piquante.

Our fourth child, Marleen, was four years old when I returned to full-time work at Tri-Parish Bank. In a career that lasted almost eighteen years, I began as file clerk and moved up the ladder to assistant vice president. I served as overdraft officer and head of customer service and data processing.

For twenty-seven years, Ernest and I worked hard at our marriage, but it failed. We divorced in 1982, when our youngest child was twelve years old. Our three older children had graduated from Eunice High School and were working and living on their own.

Ernest died suddenly and quietly in his sleep in March of 1986.

I finished raising our teenage daughter, and she too graduated from Eunice High. In 2017 all four of my children are married, own their own homes, and are financially secure. One son and one daughter live in Texas with adult children of their own. Those grandchildren have finished college, married, and are working and seeking their own American dream. My other son lives near Eunice. One daughter lives in Lafayette with three teenage children who attend French immersion schools.

I never remarried. Following my move to Lafayette in 1992, I participated at the weekly Wednesday Table Français at Dwyer's Cafe. I worked part-time and completed a paralegal and notary course, graduating with honors in 1995. I changed careers and worked in the legal field for several years, then worked part-time as a substitute teacher until my retirement in 2003.

A Table Français friend introduced me to life writing. In 2009, I signed up for the senior life writing class with the University of Louisiana at Lafayette. The sharecropping stories began as essays during my first semester. The Table Français at Dwyer's Cafe continues to be an essential part of my life in 2017.